THE INSPIRATION OF THE BIBLE

BY THE SAME AUTHOR

THE BRAZEN SERPENT
THE UNKNOWN GOD
THE REPUBLIC AND THE CHURCH
THE SIX FUNDAMENTALS OF RELIGION
THE GREAT ADVENTURE
THE GIFT OF LOVE

THE INSPIRATION OF THE BIBLE

BY

THE REV. JOHN A. McCLOREY, S. J.

B. HERDER BOOK CO.,
15 & 17 SOUTH BROADWAY, ST. LOUIS, MO.,
AND
33 QUEEN SQUARE, LONDON, W. C.
1929

Printed in U. S. A.

IMPRIMI POTEST

Die 27. Decembris, 1928,

J. J. O'Callaghan, S.J.,

Praepositus Provincialis

Provinciae Chicagiensis, S.J.

NIHIL OBSTAT

Sti. Ludovici, die 3. Martii, 1929,

H. Hussmann,

Censor Librorum

IMPRIMATUR

Sti. Ludovici, die 4. Martii, 1929,

✠ *Joannes J. Glennon,*

Archiepiscopus

Vail-Ballou Press, Inc., Binghamton and New York

To A

CONTENTS

THE INSPIRATION OF THE BIBLE

INSPIRATION OF THE BIBLE

BALTHASAR'S FEAST

"Balthasar, the king, made a great feast for a thousand of his nobles. And there were hung up on every side sky-colored green and violet hangings, fastened with cords of silk, inserted into rings of ivory and held up by marble pillars. The couches also were of gold and silver, placed in order on a floor of paved porphyry and white marble, which was embellished with paintings of wondrous variety. And they that were invited drank from golden cups and the meats were brought in divers vessels one after another. Wine also in abundance and of the best was presented as was worthy of a king's magnificence, and the guests were regaled with the sound of the trumpet, of the flute and of the harp, of the sackbut, of psaltery and symphony, and all kinds of music.

"And being now drunk, the king demanded that they should bring the vessels of gold and silver which Nabuchodonoser, his father, had carried away out of the Temple that was in Jerusalem, that the king and his nobles, his wives and concubines might drink in them. Then were the gold and silver vessels brought and the king and his courtiers, his wives and his concubines drank in them. They drank wine and praised their gods of gold and silver, of bronze, of iron, and of wood and stone. In that same hour there appeared fingers, as it were of the hand of a man, writing over against the candle sticks upon the surface of the wall of the king's palace; and the king beheld the joints of the hand that wrote. Then was the king's countenance changed, and his thoughts troubled him, and the joints of his loins were loosed, and his knees struck one against another.

"And the wise men of the king, although promised purple garments and golden chains and preëminence in the kingdom if they should read and interpret the writing, failed utterly in the attempt. Whereupon Balthasar was much troubled, and his courtiers with him. Then the king's mother reminded him of Daniel, a special favorite of the gods, full of wisdom and understanding, and proficient in the interpretation of mysteries. Forthwith the king called for Daniel and said to him: "If thou shalt read the writing and show me the interpretation of it, I will clothe thee in purple, and place a gold chain around thy neck, and make thee the third prince of my kingdom."

But Daniel made answer and said: "Thy rewards be to thyself, and the gifts of thy house give to another; but the writing I will read to thee, O King, and show thee the interpretation thereof. The Lord God gave glory and power to Nabuchodonoser thy father, so that all feared him. But because he was ungrateful and proud, he was punished. He was driven out from the habitations of men, and his heart was made like the beast's, and his dwelling was with the wild asses, and he did eat grass like an ox, and his body was wet with the dew of heaven, until he knew that the Most High rules in the kingdoms of men. Thou also, his son, hast not humbled thy heart, but hast sacrilegiously drunk wines from the sacred vessels of God and praised thy false gods, but the God who hath thy breath in his hands, and all thy ways, thou hast not praised. Wherefore he hath set the hand which has written this that is set down. And this is the writing that is written: Mane, Thecel, Phares. Mane: God hath numbered thy kingdom and finished it. Thecel; Thou art weighed in the balance and found wanting. Phares; Thy kingdom is divided and given to the Medes and Persians." Then, by the king's command, Daniel was clothed in purple, a chain of gold was placed around his neck, and it was proclaimed of him that he had power as the third man of the kingdom. That same night Balthasar the Chaldean King was slain, and Darius the Mede succeeded to the kingdom, being three score and two years old.

Daniel was a prototype of Christ; Balthasar and his court were prototypes of the Jews of Christ's time; the sacred vessels taken from Jerusalem were figures of Christ, the Vessel of Holiness; Balthasar's profanation of the golden chalices of God was a shadowy anticipation of the sacrilegious violation of the Body of Christ upon the cross; and the Chaldeans' punishment gave us an inkling of what Israel's would be.

Referring to the punishment of Israel,

Christ, with tears in His eyes, said one day to Jerusalem, the fated city of His love: "If thou hadst known the things that are unto thy peace; but now they are hidden from thy eyes. For the day shall come upon thee, and thy enemy shall cast a trench about thee, and compass thee round, and straighten thee on every side, and beat thee flat to the ground, and thy children who are in thee; and they shall not leave in thee a stone upon a stone, because thou hast not known the time of thy visitation."

And in the year seventy of the Christian era the iron men of Rome, under Vespasian and his son Titus, tired of the endless tumult and rebelliousness of the city of David, came, verifying this doleful prophecy to the letter. Nearly a million Jews perished during the siege of Jerusalem, the Temple was destroyed and the people were scattered because the City, not piously but sacrilegiously, had drunk the wine of His Blood from the sacred vessel of His Body, from Head and Feet and Hands, at the first Good Friday Feast of jealousy and hate. Christ had seen the handwriting upon the wall: Mane, Thecal, Phares; Ruin, Desolation, Death. He had read it for them, but they would not listen nor repent; so from that day to this they have been wanderers under the Judgment of God. Last year I stood at the "Wall of Wailing" in Jerusalem, watching Jews, young and old, rich and poor, with printed passages of Jeremias and Isaias in their hands, lamenting the lost glory of Israel, kissing the dear remnants of the wall of the Temple, and hoping for the day when Jerusalem will once again be the City of God and the spiritual center of the world.

There was another scene in which Christ, the real Daniel, read the handwriting upon the wall for another Balthasar, namely, the world which violates the sacred vessel of His Religion.

In St. Matthew we read: "When Jesus was seated on Mount Olivet, the disciples came to him privately and said: Tell us what shall be the sign of Thy coming and of the consummation of the world. And Jesus answering said to them: Nation shall rise against nation and kingdom against kingdom, and there shall be pestilences and famines and earthquakes in places. Now these are the beginnings of sorrows. And immediately after the tribulation of those days the sun shall be darkened, and the moon shall not give her light, and the stars shall fall from heaven, and the powers of heaven shall be moved. And then shall appear the sign of the Son of Man in heaven and all tribes of the earth shall mourn, and they shall see the Son of Man coming in the clouds of heaven in much power and majesty. And He shall send his angels with a trumpet and a great voice, and they shall gather together His elect from the four winds, from the farthest part of heaven to the utmost bounds of them. And all nations shall be gathered before Him and He shall separate them one from another as the Shepherd separateth the sheep from the goats and He shall set the sheep on His right but the goats on His left."

"Mane, Thecel, Phares!" Christ said and still says to the festive rebellious world, sacrilegiously rejecting Him and His Christianity and adoring its false gods of gold and silver, brass, wood and stone: "If you do not repent, you shall stand before the Judgment Seat at the end of the world and hear this sentence: Depart from me ye cursed into everlasting fire, prepare for the devil and his angels."

The third Daniel, the Church, Christ's successor and representative upon earth, reads the handwriting upon the wall for Modernism, the latest Balthasar; because Modernism has violated the sacred vessel of the Bible by pouring out upon the ground the delicious wine of God's written Word and replacing it with draughts of rationalistic interpretation for the lips of the vain and irreverent.

Modernists have taken the Bible from the sanctuary of the Church, where it had always been in honor like the sacred vessels in the Holy of Holies of the Temple, have stripped it of its divine prerogatives, and lowered it to the level of a merely human composition full of myths, legends, folklore, popular traditions, errors, lies, and immorality.

Hence our religion and civilization, largely built upon the bible, are falling to pieces. The fundamental lesson of the bible is one God, Creator of Heaven and earth. A group of contemporaneous Modernists, named Association for the Advancement of Atheism, call the God of the bible a Moloch and are spreading their atheistic tenets in our high schools, colleges, and universities.

The second lesson of the bible is that of the Son of God in human flesh dying to atone for the sins of man. These bible haters say that Christ is only a man, like Socrates or Plato, that atonement implies a blood-thirsty, vengeful deity, that sin is a myth, and that the perverse wickedness of human nature is not attributable to the fall of Adam, but to our origin in beasts, from whose brutishness we are gradually evolving into a state of human virtue.

The third lesson of the bible is that of man, the adopted son of God, a spiritual and immortal being. Evolutionary Modernists would put him down from the throne of his spirituality; and if they had their way, man, like Nabuchodonser, would be driven out, his heart made like the beast's, his dwelling would be among the wild asses, he would eat grass like the ox, and his body would be wet from the dew of heaven;—or rather, to speak more exactly, he would inhabit trees, swing from branches, eat nuts, chatter and live by his claws and tail.

Murder, covetousness, impurity and luxury received from the bible a stigma which made them terrible things; but those vices have become quite tolerable since the bible has gone.

The murderous violence of the United States has made us a by-word among the nations. In Detroit, for instance, murder has become a diversion. Brave up-standing policemen are shot down by crooks without receiving much sympathy from the same sort of people who used to weep over the courage and sufferings of soldiers. Sob-sisters, male and female, have abolished the great deterrent to murder; *i. e.,* a greased rope and a six-foot fall; because, forsooth, they pity the poor, dear criminals, and are pitiless towards innocent civilians; and because they cannot understand that the old principle: "An eye for an eye, a tooth for a tooth, and a life for a life," when reposed in the hands of the calm judicial State, is not vengeful cruelty, but majestic justice. Then lawyers, proficient in juggling legal technicalities, impede court sentences and save murderers from just punishment. Moreover, life sentences are seldom for life; there is always the hope of release. Steps have already been taken to deliver young King of Battle Creek, Michigan, from the punishment for his brutal assault; and the two murderers of the Frank boy of Chicago still hope to be freed.

If murder were confined to the offscouring of society, it would not be so regrettable. But what shall we think of murder, committed in the name of the Federal Government and apparently condoned! A few months ago two dastardly fellows, under the ægis of Columbia, without reason cruelly murdered a man and a little girl in the Detroit river in the all-holy name of the deity Prohibition. A flare of indignation swept across Detroit at the time, but silence soon fell, the press has been mute for months, and no punishment has been meted out to the miscreants, because dry fanaticism, like a nightmare, sits on the prostrate form of Liberty. I yield to no man in patriotism; but I do object to the prohibitionist's belief that the Constitution of the United States is above the Ten Commandments. These men, with few exceptions, have nothing to say against murder committed in the name of Prohibition, against insulting references to Christianity made by a State University President, against birth control and divorce; but they whip themselves into a fury of indignation against violators of the liquor law. Some sins are wrong, not because they are forbidden; rather they are forbidden because they are essentially and eternally wrong; for instance, murder and divorce. But other acts, not evil in themselves, are wrong only because they are forbidden; for instance the manufacture, transportation and sale of liquor in the United States. There is a whole world of difference, therefore, between the legislation of Mount Sinai and that of Washington, D. C.; and it is about time for Prohibitionists to get a right perspective of wrongdoing and stop overemphasizing the man-made law against liquor to the neglect of the God-made and nature-made law against murder, divorce, birth control, unjust business, and sinful luxury.

In view of the murderous violence now rampant amongst us, the pendulum of legislation has naturally swung from the extreme of laxity to the opposite extreme of ruthlessness. So we have had in Michigan the case of a man imprisoned for life for four felonies which did not deserve such severity. According to the press two of his offences were drinking liquor, a third was counterfeiting money, and a fourth was porch climbing unarmed. It is grimly ironical to see a poor fellow sent up for life for drinking gin, while gin-drinking and gin-selling Federal Officers kill girls and go free, while divorcees retain their position in respectable society, while Sybarites indulge in natural and unnatural crimes, and conscienceless capitalists absorb the wealth of the world.

Divorce is now an accepted form of normality in America. I will not tell you how wide spread it is, for you know that as well as I. This cancer is polluting our people and will be the ruin of the nation. Government is built upon families; if families fail, the government will topple. But divorce is a mortal thrust at the family. If women deteriorate, men will decay, for the level of morality among men depends on its level among women. People call women the weaker sex. Absurd! Women are stronger than men, and men's conduct is regulated by theirs. But divorce debauches women. The child is the hope of the race. Marriage is perpetual chiefly for the protection of the child. Therefore, divorce is death to the child and the race. A friend of mine met a

Jap in Europe last year and asked him if the Japanese were trying to overthrow the United States. The Oriental smiled quizzically and said: "No, we are waiting for the United Staes to overthrow itself."[2] He meant, among other things, divorce.

Birth control has become respectable and scientific. Appealing as it does to the strongest passion of the heart, it has been gaining an easy and widespread victory. And it is so plausible! Health and safety of mothers, improved quality of offspring, limited food supplies of the world, moderate income, these and ten other such reasons for birth control are only a hair's breadth from the truth. A hair's breadth, of course, makes the whole difference between the sublimest truth and the foulest error. But the birth controllers are not keen-eyed enough to see the slender line of demarcation between the two extremes.

The Industrial Revolution of a hundred and fifty years ago took away from workingmen, against their will, their tools, raw material, and individual craftsmanship, thus making the owners of machinery economically omnipotent. Aside from the possible justice or injustice of individual capitalists, the capitalistic system itself, monopolizing as it does the means of production, is unjust. For it has absorbed into itself the tools, raw material and individual craftsmanship of workingmen without making adequate return for the spoliation. Thus capitalists possess an undue power in dictating to labor, and, for that matter, even to the government. Since a return to the old order of individual production, which prevailed before the Industrial Revolution, is not feasible nor desired even by the most radical, some other method of placing Capital and Labor in a less unjust relationship must be devised. The partial ownership of the means of production by Labor would solve the problem. Two weapons of defence which workingmen have not yet lost, are the right to unionize and strike, although attempts to rob them of these have been made by some greedy capitalists. Naturally enough, workingmen have abused their weapons by creating the walking delegate and the closed shop, by frittering their time away, by demanding exorbitant wages for little work, by palming off inefficient employees upon just and generous employers. We must blame them for this, but at the same time we must not forget that the capitalistic monopoly of wealth has occasioned it. Other baneful results of the accumulation of vast wealth in the hands of a few individuals are wild and sumptuous extravagance, luxurious softness of character, and vulgar display.

These are some of the fruits of the sacrilegious violation of the sacred vessel of the bible. On the bible our morality is largely built. The destructive criticism of the bible by Modernists has been the ruin of our morality. The ruin of the nation will inevitably follow; for a nation without one God, Creator of Heaven and Earth, without Jesus Christ, the Saviour of men, and without man considered as a spiritual and immortal being, a nation permeated by murder, divorce, birth control, excessive wealth, unjust business, and widespread poverty must fall.

And so the handwriting is upon the wall. Modernists, engaged in draining the bible of the last drop of the supernatural, do not see the menacing words; nevertheless, they are there; for God is just and holy, He will not be mocked, nor have His book mocked. Every morning I look at the roseate dawn and tremble to see Mane, Thecel, Phares written on the wall of the eastern sky. I gaze at the midnight stars, and Mane, Thecel, Phares burn on the ceiling of the world. Etched on mountain sides the three horrible words confront me, on the surface of rivers and lakes I see them flame, and amid the din and clamor of the busy city as well as in the still small hours of sleep and dreaming, I hear Mane, Thecel, Phares, spoken to my dear country in punishment for the sins of her Modernistic children; God hath numbered thy kingdom and finished it. Thou art weighed in the balance and found wanting. Thy kingdom is divided and given to the Medes and Persians.

The story of Balthasar's feast closes with the smashing short sentence: "The same night Balthasar, the Chaldean king, was slain, and Darius the Mede succeeded to the kingdom." I also will end as briefly as I can. Columbia will fall. Her enemies will build on her ruins. A foreign flag, whether Asiatic or European, will top our ships, city buildings and fortresses, and we in defeat shall mourn our lost glory. The old kings will come back with a ha ha at the failure of democracy and the first-born republic of modern times will be only a memory,—a memory of youth, strength, beauty and promise, blighted suddenly because the sacred vessel of the bible was taken from the sanctuary of the Church and defiled by the sacrilegious hands of revellers, drunk with intellectual conceit at the banquet board of Modernistic theology.

THE CANONICITY OF THE BIBLE

Last Sunday night I prophesied dolors for America. My prophecy, however, was only conditional. America will fall if the bible continues to be scorned. But if people come to their senses, respect the bible, and accept its lessons of one God, Creator of heaven and earth, Jesus Christ, His Only Son, and man considered as a spiritual and immortal being; if they avoid murder, divorce, birth control, excessive wealth, sinful luxury and unjust business;—the handwriting upon the wall will be erased, God's wrath will be appeased, Daniel will revoke his judgment, the Medes and Persians will not come, America will be saved. So I imagine you, true lovers of your country, resolving henceforth to respect the bible.

However, some of you may be asking in your mind, what are these arguments of Modernists against Holy Writ, and what are the answers of the Church? Such questions are fair, and I shall try to answer them. Therefore, the five following lectures of this course will be on the Canonicity, Inspiration, Infallible Truth, Partial Obscurity and Insufficiency of Holy Writ, and the Relation of the bible of Tradition.

The inspiration of Sacred Scripture is on every tongue to-day. In drawing rooms, class rooms, and on street corners we hear that the Old Testament is a myth, a popular exaggeration of facts. People do not believe, for instance, that Adam was the first man, that Eve was taken from his side, that both of them were placed in the garden of delights, where they were tempted by the devil in the form of a serpent and sinned, whence they were expelled with the punishment of original sin upon themselves and their progeny for all time. People do not believe that the earth and the human race are as young as Scripture says, that the world was made in six days, that there was a universal flood, that God came down from heaven, confusing the speech of the builders of Babel, that the Red Sea parted for Moses and his followers, that manna fell from heaven, that the whale swallowed Jonah, that prophets foretold future events, that angels fought at the side of Judas Macchabees, accompanied Tobias and that Daniel was unharmed in the lion's den. People do not believe that Christ worked miracles to prove His divinity, nor even that He claimed to be divine. On the contrary, they do believe in Darwinian evolution, which certainly contradicts the bible. Is this not a fair statement of the talk that goes on every day around us?

The cause of this popular scepticism is Modernism. Modernism contains three essential errors, concerned with knowledge, faith, and dogmatic expression. For while the Church teaches that we can by abstract thinking rise from a knowledge of the physical world round about us to a knowledge of the deity; and from history can know miracles, supernatural revelation and Christ's divinity: Modernists hold with Immanuel Kant that we cannot come to a knowledge of God from the physical world, and that history, being a record of purely natural events, can give us no evidence of Christ's divinity.

Second, while the Church teaches that the *object* of faith is a known fact in the objective order, that the *channel* of faith is objective supernatural revelation, confirmed by miracles; and that *faith* itself is an act, partly of the intellect and partly of the will: Modernists hold that the *object* of faith is a group of personal feelings and imaginations by which we idealize facts; by which, for instance, we exaggerate the Man Christ into a God-Man, just as the pagans of old used to enlarge a human hero into a demigod;—feelings and imaginations which are *not preceded* by ideas, but arise from a blind impulse of the heart. They hold that the *channel* of faith (revelation) is not objective, but subjective, *i. e.,* our consciousness of our religious feelings and imaginations, and that *faith* itself is this consciousness.

Third, while the Church teaches that dogmatic propositions express an objective fact and are, therefore, eternally true and unchangeable, because whatever is done can never be undone, what was thus and so in the past can never be otherwise: Modernists hold that the truth of dogmatic expression consists in faithfully uttering one's religious feelings and imaginations about facts; and that, therefore, since with the passing of centuries the religious feelings and imaginations of the individual and the community become more perfect, the dogmatic expressions of a former age may not satisfy the religious feelings and imaginations of the new age, hence will cease to be true and ought to be changed.

So much for Modernism in general. It is obvious that Modernism, applied to Scripture, means that the bible is not a record of facts, but only of its authors' feelings and imaginations about facts. Hence the bible is full of myths, legends, folk-lore, personal idealizations, subjective exaggerations of facts. For instance, the Christ of St. John's Gospel was in reality a mere man; He was a God Man only in St. John's mystical dreams of Him. Because Scripture, especially the New Testament, is probably the best expression of the best religious feelings of the world, which we in our personal religious experiences will very likely never surpass, it follows that Scripture will almost certainly always be true. But if at some future date we should chance to elicit higher feelings than those of Scripture, the expressions of Scripture will not meet the need of our religious feelings and, therefore, will cease to be true.

The excess of Modernism has quite naturally occasioned an excess in the opposite direction. The trial at Dayton, Tennessee, is a fair illustration of Fundamentalism at its worst,—belief in extreme scriptural literalism. Fundamentalists, imagining that the authors of the Old Testament wrote with a scientific exactness which characterizes histories of to-day; making no allowances for the naïve style of narrative, undoubtedly prevalent in those olden days, have by their narrow-minded interpretation laid Scripture open to attacks from evolution and similar sciences. And so, many who accept evolution feel constrained to reject Holy Writ.

It is fitting, therefore, that, in the midst of these contradictory scriptural views, the golden mean should be explained. I shall make the attempt, and in doing so shall fall back upon the authority of the Church.

In this lecture it is only assumed (not proved) that the Church is infallible when teaching *ex cathedra.* We cannot prove everything at once. Possibly on some future occasion the infallibility of the Church will be explained. We assume, moreover, but do not prove, that Holy Writ in part is an historical document; we wish to prove only that it is inspired. The distinction between historicity and inspiration is obvious. An historical document need not be inspired, for instance, Guizot's History of France. An inspired document need not be historical, for instance, the poems of the bible. On a former occasion the historical character of the four Gospels was established; and indeed even Rationalists believe they are authentic beyond doubt. Now what is true of the Gospels, is true also of other Scriptural books which the Church holds to be historical.

You will observe, when you read the Declaration of the Council of Trent on Scripture, that explicitly there is question only of the canonicity of the bible. But implicitly also its inspiration is affirmed; because, although canonicity and inspiration are distinct ideas, in the concrete they are one and the same thing. A book is inspired if it is the Word of God; a book is canonical if it is acknowledged by the Church as the Word of God. It is obvious, then, that inspiration is inherent in an inspired book, whereas canonicity is extrinsic to it and subsequent to its inspiration. As a matter of fact, according to the Council of Trent, all canonical books are inspired, all inspired books are canonical.

The Declaration of the Council of Trent,

from which our proof is taken, is the following: "If anyone says that all the books (Protocanonical and Deuterocanonical) of both Testaments with all their parts, as they are read in the Catholic Church and contained in the old Latin Vulgate edition, are not sacred and canonical, let him be anathema!"

The Protocanonical Books of the bible are those about whose sacred and inspired character no doubt was ever entertained in the Church. Deuterocanonical are those about whose sacred and inspired character a doubt was entertained by some Catholics for a time, though it was never sufficient to hurt the practically unanimous judgment of the Fathers in favor of the Deuterocanonical books. Apocryphal books are those which some few people for a short time considered to be sacred and inspired but which are now certainly known not to be such. The Protos are all the books of the Old Testament except Judith, Wisdom, Ecclesiasticus, parts of Daniel, Baruch, Esther in parts, Tobias and the two books of Macchabees. In the New Testament, St. Paul's Epistle to the Hebrews, St. James and Jude's Epistles, the second epistle of St.

Peter, the second and third epistles of St. John, and the Apocalypse. Obviously the Deuteros are the books just named.

Translators of the King James authorized Protestant bible excluded the Deuterocanonical books of the Old Testament from the canon, considering them to be apocryphal; 1st, because St. Jerome did so; 2nd because the Hebrew Old Testament did not contain them; 3rd, because Christ and the Apostles never quoted from them, and 4th, because Josephus, the great Hebrew historian, did not include them in his canon. But St. Jerome was too deferential to the Hebrews, among whom he studied, and his single adverse opinion is of little value against the almost universal judgment of the Fathers of the Church. Moreover, St. Jerome's opposition to the Deuterocanonical books was wavering; and while he speculated on their spurious character, in practice he accepted them as genuine and inspired. True, the Deuterocanonical books are not contained in the Hebrew Old Testament as we have it now. But that is nothing against them, as we shall see presently. If the argument from Christ's silence and that of the Apostles is a valid one, some of the

Protocanonical books which Protestants admit to be inspired, are not such, because Christ and the Apostles did not quote from two of these. The authority of Josephus is weakened by the fact that he regarded some fables as histories; moreover, he at times refers to the Deuterocanonical books as divine.

Protestants at one time or other regarded the Epistle to the Hebrews as apocryphal because it differs widely in style from St. Paul's other letters; and Luther said that St. James' Epistle on practical works of charity is a "straw letter" because it was opposed to his own doctrine of justification by faith without good works. But St. Paul's letter to the Hebrews, though his own in thought and sentiment, was composed by his secretary; and Luther's a priori argument against St. James' letter is based on the false supposition that his doctrine of justification by faith without good works is true.

In times past certain Catholic theologians thought that only those portions of the bible are sacred and inspired which deal with faith and morals. They ventured the opinion that, since the Church is infallible only in regard to faith and morals, she can give us assurance of the inspiration of the bible only when the bible treats of faith and morals. This, however, is not true. For since, as even Protestants admit, the whole inspiration of Scripture is a matter of faith, the Church can pronounce infallibly upon the inspiration of the most insignificant sentence of the Holy Book.

Cardinal Newman taught that at least the "obiter dicta" of Holy Writ, *i. e.,* insignificant trifles, were not inspired, because it would have been unworthy of the Deity to inspire them. But when it comes to the question of worthiness or unworthiness, we must admit that it was unworthy of God, in a sense, to write Scripture at all, to become man and die for us on the cross.

So much for the inspiration of the bible, as it was when it first proceeded from the hand of God in its original languages. But what of translations and possible textual corruptions?

It was possible, of course, for God to inspire translators of the bible, so that as a consequence every word of theirs would be infallibly true. But as a matter of fact the translators were *not* divinely inspired. Hence their writings are God's word only in the sense that the originals from which they were made, were inspired and had God as their author.

The Septuagint was a Greek translation of the Old Testament made about three centuries B. C. for the benefit of Alexandrian Jews, who had forgotten Hebrew. According to tradition, Ptolemy II Philadelphus, king of Egypt, having heard of the wonderful Hebrew book and wishing to make it accessible in his library at Alexandria, requested the authorities at Jerusalem to lend him some learned men to do the Hebrew into Greek. Seventy men were sent, who, placed in seventy separate cells, finished the work piecemeal in seventy days. Hence "Septuagint," which is the Greek word for seventy.

The Deuterocanonical books are contained in the Septuagint, but not in the Hebrew Old Testament as we have it to-day. But that proves nothing against them; for God could have inspired the human authors to compose in Greek or some other language as well as in Hebrew; as in fact He did. Hence the translators of the Septuagint took the books of Judith, Esther in parts, Tobias and the two books of the Machabees, etc., as they found them in their original gentile tongue, and incorporated them into their Greek translation of the Hebrew Old Testament. It is worthy of note that Christ and the Apostles quoted most frequently from the Septuagint; seldom from the Hebrew Old Testament.

The Old Latin Itala was a Latin translation whose Old Testament was taken from the Septuagint, whose New Testament was derived from the Greek and Aramaic in which languages the New Testament was originally composed. It was in vogue in the Western Church up to the time of St. Jerome, when Pope Damasus, observing that many corruptions had crept into it, ordered that Saint to make a new translation.

The Vulgate, so called because, from the time of St. Jerome up to the Reformation, it was regarded by the Western Church as the authentic version, is the work of St. Jerome. St. Jerome took the Protocanonical books of the Old Testament mostly from the ancient Hebrew. The Deuterocanonical books of the Old Testament he took from the Old Latin and corrected them. He took the New Testament also from the Old Latin, corrected it and made critical comparisons with the Greek and Aramaic texts.

The Douay version, commonly used in English-speaking countries, was done at Douay in Belgium about four hundred years ago by a group of English exiles under Cardinal Allen. The King James version is a Protestant translation of the bible made under James I of England. Its sources are the Bishop's bible, a translation made by the Protestant bishop Parker and his confrères under Queen Elizabeth, the Great Bible made at the instance of Cromwell, a minion of Henry VIII, the Matthew bible made by Coverdale, Tyndale's translation and the Vulgate, Old Latin (not the Septuagint), Hebrew Old Testament and Erasmus's Greek Text of the New Testament.

Are all the books of the bible with all their parts, as they were contained in the Vulgate in the sixteenth century, sacred and inspired? It is obvious that the possibility of mistranslation and textual corruption makes this quite a different question from the preceding one about the inspiration of the bible as it was when it first proceeded from the hand of God in its original languages.

To these two questions about the inspiration of the bible, 1st, in its original languages and, 2nd, in the Vulgate translation in the sixteenth century, at the time the Council of Trent, the Church answers by the canonical declaration given above.

In saying that all the parts of the Vulgate are inspired, the Council of Trent referred in particular to three portions about whose inspiration there had been some doubt among Catholics; *i. e.,* the Bloody Sweat in St. Luke, the story of the woman taken in sin in St. John, and a portion of the last chapter of St. Mark.

It must be remembered that the words, "The bible with all its parts is inspired," do not refer to a multitude of slight corruptions (not touching on faith, morals, substantial history or even the integrity of any single chapter of the bible) which in the course of centuries have crept into the Vulgate on account of the difficulty of transcribing texts by hand in numberless copies, some of the manuscripts being almost illegible. These mistakes concern punctuation, spelling, grammar, transposition of words, and even changes of whole sentences. A miracle would have been required to avoid such errors, and we have no right to expect that God would work a miracle for the preservation of biblical integrity in regard to unimportant minutiae. In the Catholic and Protestant bibles alike the number of such unimportant variants runs up into the thousands.

There is no evidence in the bible itself that the whole bible is inspired. True, Christ and the Apostles said that the whole Old Testament is inspired, but it is not clear from their statements precisely which books constitute the Old Testament. True, too, they explicitly affirmed that some particular Old Testament books were inspired; but among these were not the Deuteros nor two of the Protos. However some allusions of Christ show that He favored the Deuteros; and the Apostles referring to the Greek Old Testament drew no distinction between Protos and Deuteros. The scriptural evidence for the inspiration of the New Testament is even less. True, St. Paul tells Timothy that all scripture inspired by God is useful. But it is obvious that the great Apostle was referring to the Old Testament, from which Timothy had learned at his mother's knee. Besides some portions of the New Testament were not yet in existence when the letter to Timothy was composed. True St. Peter declares that St. Paul's letters were inspired. But aside from the fact that St. Peter's epistle giving this favorable testimony to the letters of St. Paul has been rejected by most Protestants as spurious, the reference would not prove the inspiration of the whole New Testament. St. Luke and St. John seem to imply that the Acts of the Apostles and the Apocalypse were inspired; but what of the inspiration of the four Gospels, which form the nucleus of the New Testament? Most Protestants and some Catholics have said the Apostolate necessarily implies inspiration. Is that true?

Negatively it is true in the sense that nothing written after Apostolic times is inspired. But is it true positively, in the sense, for example, that simply because the Gospels of St. Matthew and St. John were composed by Apostles, *therefore* they were inspired by God? This is far from certain. True, the Apostolate implies *revelation* and *infallibility,* because to the Apostles was committed the revelation of God, and they were preserved by a special gift of infallibility from making mistakes in preaching it. But, as we shall see in a later lecture of this course, *revelation* and *infallibility* are quite different things from *inspiration.* But even if the Apostolate did imply inspiration, the inspiration of the Gospels of Mark and Luke would still be unproved and unprovable from the bible, for the simple reason that Mark and Luke were not Apostles.

For these reasons it is clear that the Church draws her evidence for the inspiration of the *whole* bible from Tradition, the spoken word of Christ or the Apostles, come down to us from Apostolic times through the Fathers and ancient councils of the Church. That Tradition is a reliable source of divine knowledge, we shall see in the last lecture of the course. Assuming now as true what we shall then prove to be true, we say that in the Fathers the Church finds the universally taught doctrine that the whole bible without exception is inspired. This doctrine, the Fathers declare, came down to them from the Apostles. Obviously they meant to include the Deuterocanonical books in their general assertion. For the Western

Fathers up to the time of St. Jerome used the Old Latin translation; while the Eastern Fathers used the Septuagint. But both these versions contained the Deuteros in an equal place of honor with the Protos. In the beginning of the fourth century the Council of Carthage taking its cue from the Fathers, included the Deuteros in its canon. Now the Church, in comparing her Vulgate translation of the sixteenth century with the Fathers' versions, saw that they substantially agreed. Moreover our Douay and Vulgate translations of to-day are identical with the Vulgate of the sixteenth century. Therefore, we can say with complete assurance that our Bible of to-day is sacred, canonical, and inspired in all its parts.

Here, then, Brethren, you have a true picture of the Catholic Church giving to the modern world a most precious thing, the holy bible. The bible was not one book from the beginning. The Church made it one. The different books of the Bible were written in different languages, centuries, and places; they were enclosed under different covers, scattered through the world, mixed up and confused with a multitude of apocryphal works, spurious scriptures, forged gospels which claimed the same divine authorship as the genuine books of the bible. It was the Church that drew order out of chaos, unity out of multiplicity, by rejecting the apocrypha and collecting the genuine books of Scripture into one volume. It was the Church that assured men that the bible is not a forgery, that preserved it from substantial corruption down through the centuries, that satisfied us as to its inspiration, that guarded it against false translations and thus handed it down whole and entire to the modern world.

Yet some Protestants snatch it from her, as it were, boasting of their devotion to it and accusing her of neglecting it. The Church, they say, substitutes herself for the bible. She does not. According to her own doctrine it is her office to explain the bible. Catholics, they say, prefer the Church to the bible. We do not. We only prefer the Church's interpretation of it to Protestants' personal opinion of it. They say that the Church chained the bible. So she did, because, being copied by hand with exquisite care and illuminated with choicest artistic beauty, the bible, like a picture of Raphael, was a treasure likely to be stolen. They say that before the Reformation Catholics did not read the bible. In St. Jerome's day Catholics knew the New Testament by heart. In later centuries they did not read the bible for the simple reason that they could not read at all and because, before the introduction of printing, copies of the bible were scarce. But, as Ruskin said, the Church made up for these defects by embodying Scriptural truths in stained-glass windows, marbles, and canvases. Even after the introduction of printing the Church objected to false translations of the bible and to reading it without her guidance, merely out of curiosity or to criticise. Before Luther's German translation there were one hundred and ninety-eight versions of the bible in the popular languages of Europe. In modern days, Leo XIII encouraged Catholic lay people to read it; and Pius X condemned Modernism for its attacks on Holy Writ, established the biblical Institute at Rome for the exhaustive study of the bible, and appointed the biblical Commission to pronounce on the value of modern books on Scripture.

On the contrary (and I trust that my separated brethren will not think that this is being said in a spirit of animosity) in the hands of Protestants during the past few centuries the bible has given birth to a host of contradictory doctrines and is to-day being stripped of all divine authority by those who declare that they did not give up the Pope of Rome to become slaves of "a paper Pope."

Protestants say that they think for themselves, whereas Catholics submit to authority. A railroad train might as well boast of running for and by itself without tracks and the guiding hand of the engineer. The Church does not save us from the trouble of thinking, but only from the trouble of thinking recklessly: just as railroad tracks do not prevent a train from running, but from running into a ditch. Free thought is as unnatural and ruinous as free love. A directing and constraining channel for thought is as necessary as banks for a stream. The banks, the channel, make the whole difference between a useful current and a destructive flood. The Mississippi inundation was symbolic of modern thought breaking barriers and running riot. It is more interesting of course to pursue truth for oneself. But the capture, not the mere pursuit of truth, is the end and object of life. Catholics with the help of the Church have captured Scriptural truth. Can non-Catholics say as much for private judgment? Then how few Protestants with all their boasted private judgment have stopped to exercise it on the Church's claim to authority? Non-Catholics accept the authoritative teachings of doctors, lawyers, business men, and scientists. Why do they stop short at the authority of the Church? Surely the science of religion requires the expert treatment of specialists no less than other sciences. Surely the man in the street cannot settle questions of religion more easily than those of profane arts and sciences.

But the Church is more than a teacher; she is also a spouse, brooding for centuries in contemplative tenderness over the recorded sayings and doings of Christ, her heroic Beloved. Youthful forever, beautiful without blemish, the Mother of Fair Love, she sits with the book in her lap, telling her children at her knee over and over again the story of Christ, their Father and her Spouse. We Catholics belong to an ancient House whose Founder established it at the price of His blood. The Church was present when He accomplished this gigantic feat. She lives on the memory of it, and she would draw our thoughts and affections from a thousand distractions to the altitude which He scaled. If we try to interpret the story of Him by ourselves, without the personal touch of this contemporaneous witness, we shall misconstrue the record; but if we contemplate Him through her eyes, through the eyes of one who was present and saw and heard and loved, we shall vision Him aright, saturate our souls with His beauty, and embody Him forth in our lives.

THE INSPIRATION OF THE BIBLE

Last week we studied the canonicity of Sacred Scripture; to-night we shall consider its inspiration. Then we asked which are the inspired books of the bible; now we ask, in what precisely does inspiration consist?

The word Inspiration can mean twenty different things. For instance, we say that Shakespeare, Dante, and Plato were inspired. That means that they were highly poetical. We say that Napoleon Bonaparte inspired the French people to do heroic deeds. That means only that he was magnetic in character. We say, I got an inspiring thought from reading Thomas à Kempis, or St. Augustine's City of God, or the Life of the Little Flower. That means only that we were enriched with a pious emotion or enlightening idea. We say that a man is inspired with love for a woman. That means only that he has been the victim of infatuation. Then the word "inspired" is a derivative from the Latin word "spiritus," which signifies a "wind" or a "breath"; and so suggests the idea of a soul driven like a sail-boat before the wind of heaven; the idea of God breathing the soul of the first man into a body of dust; the idea of Christ breathing power into His Apostles when He sent them forth for the conversion of the world; the idea of the Holy Spirit descending on the Apostles on Pentecost in the form of a great wind and fiery tongues.

And so to an independent thinker the inspiration of Scripture could have a variety of meanings. But what does Scriptural inspiration signify in reality? For the answer we shall fall back on the authority of the Church.

The four sources from which the argument will be drawn are the Council of the Vatican, the Scriptural Letter of Leo XIII, Pius X's Letter against the Modernists, and a declaration or two of the Biblical Commission.

The statement of the Vatican Council runs as follows: "The Church considers the books of the bible sacred and canonical, not because they were composed only by human industry and afterwards approved by her authority, nor only because they contain revelation without error; but because, written under the inspiration of the Holy Ghost, they have God as their author and as such have been committed to the Church."

From this declaration of the Council it is obvious that inspiration contains five elements,—two positive and three negative. The positive elements are: "written under the inspiration of the Holy Ghost" and "as such committed to the Church." The negative elements are: the approval of the Church, infallibility, and revelation; *i. e.*, the bible is not inspired because it has been approved by the Church, nor because it is infallible, nor because it contains revelation.

Ecclesiastical approbation does not make the bible inspired. It only makes us *know* that the bible is inspired. For the approval of the Church is subsequent to the inspiration of Scripture; and therefore cannot constitute it. The approval of a document by a competent agency confers upon it an additional authority, but does not affect its authorship. For instance, if the President of the United States signs a state paper composed by his secretary, the paper is forthwith backed by the president's authority, but its authorship still belongs to the secretary. And so if Scripture had been composed by human industry and then approved by the Church, Scripture would be endowed with the Church's authority, but not with her authorship. But although the Church's approval does not constitute the inspiration of the bible, it is a necessary condition that the bible may serve its essential purpose of enlightening the faithful through the instrumentality of an infallible interpreter.

Infallibility is not inspiration. According to Catholic doctrine the pope is infallible in his teachings in matters of faith and morals to and for the whole Church; because we believe that in such circumstances God saves the pope from falling into error. But, though infallible, the pope is not inspired, because his teaching, after all, is only man's word, not God's. It is not God's word; for as Catholics and Protestants alike admit, God's word, *i. e.*, inspired teaching for the whole Church, came to a close with the death of St. John the Evangelist. But, although infallibility does not constitute inspiration, nevertheless an inspired book must be infallible because, having been written by God, who is Infinite Wisdom and Truthfulness and can neither deceive nor be deceived, it must be true. This, therefore, is plain: Scripture is not inspired because it is infallible; Scripture is infallible because it is inspired.

Revelation is not inspiration. A *revealed* truth is one which Almighty God supernaturally manifests to a passively recipient individual. A revealed truth in the strict sense of revelation was not known and in some cases could never have been known by the human individual before the revelation came; *e. g.*, the revealed truth of the Blessed Trinity. In revelation the purpose of manifesting the revealed truth to others is not essentially contained. For a truth can be manifested to a single individual exclusively for his own personal advantage. Moreover, if the revealed truth is intended for publication, it may be expressed by the recipient without inspiration, by means of his natural powers. For instance, I in this pulpit tonight, without any special inspiration from on high, am preaching the supernaturally revealed doctrine of "Scriptural Inspiration."

An *inspired* truth, on the contrary, is one which a man writes or speaks, acting simply as an instrument in God's hand; so that the resulting composition is not his, but God's.

An inspired truth could have been known and in many parts of Scripture was known before the inspiration came. For instance, the Acts of the Apostles in which St. Luke, under the special inspiration of the Holy Ghost, wrote of things which he himself had perceived by his natural powers in his travels with St. Paul. That in inspiration the purpose of manifesting the inspired truth to others is necessarily contained, is obvious. For inspiration means "writing" or "speaking," and writing or speaking of its very nature is for others. Thus it is clear that a document can be 1st, neither revealed nor inspired; for example, the plays of Shakespeare in which that great author, without any special inspiration from the Holy Ghost, wrote of things which he himself had perceived by his natural powers; 2nd, revealed but not inspired; for example, the writings of the Fathers, in which without any special inspiration of the Holy Ghost, they treated of revealed doctrines; 3rd, inspired but not revealed; *e. g.*, the Gospel of St. Mark, in which, under the inspiration of the Holy Ghost, he narrated things which he himself had perceived or of which he had heard; 4th, revealed and inspired; for example, the Gospel of St. John, in which, under the inspiration of the Holy Ghost, he wrote of the Word in the bosom of the Father from all eternity and in time made flesh; a revelation made to him by Christ.

These, therefore, are the three negative elements in the definition of the Vatican Council: the bible is not inspired because it has been approved by the Church, or because it is infallible, or because it contains revelation without error.

But there are negative factors in inspiration besides those mentioned by the Vatican Council; for instance, personal inspiration. The bible is not inspired because it inspires holy thoughts and emotions in its readers. For, aside from the fact that, according to Christ, the Apostles, the Fathers and the Church, Scriptural inspiration is something inherent to the bible, not subsequent to it and an effect of it in the reader's mind, it is questionable whether so-called personal inspirations are really from the Holy Spirit. Possibly they come from the reader himself, for auto-suggestion is a common phenomenon. Possibly they are diabolical. For the devil often assumes the semblance of an angel of light. And surely the diverse and contradictory doctrines drawn from the bible by the Protestant reformers are the strongest argument against the genuine character of their illuminations and inspirations.

The natural genius of an author does not make his book inspired. Shakespeare was a genius, and God helped him to write his plays; for without God's aid nobody could do anything. But whereas God employed St. Matthew merely as an instrument in composing the Gospel of that name, so that the Gospel was not principally Matthew's, but God's; Shakespeare, on the contrary, was the principal author of his plays, God only having concurred with him in their composition. Besides, many parts of Scripture are not works of genius at all, *e.g.*, the Book of Numbers of the Old Testament. Hence according to the doctrine that inspiration consists in the natural genius of an author, that Book was not God's word at all; a conclusion which no Catholic and few Protestants would admit to be true.

Modernistic inspiration is not Scriptural inspiration. For while the latter is the infallible and unchangeable divine expression of objective truths, the former is only the human, mutable and possibly false, expression of the human writers' blind religious feelings about objective truths.

The divine movement of the human author's will, to the exclusion of his intellect and faculty of expression, is not sufficient for inspiration. For if God moves only the will of the human author without influencing his intellect, the resulting book will not be God's; for a book is the expression of an intellect; and if God does not preserve His human instrument from erroneous expression by a special gift of infallibility, the latter may state more or less than God wishes him to express. As a consequence, readers of the bible will not know whether or not they are getting God's thoughts.

Singleness of literal meaning is necessary for Scriptural inspiration. That a text of Scripture may have a symbolic meaning over and above its literal signification is admitted by all. For instance, the sentence: "Moses led the Hebrews from Egypt into the promised land," literally means that he did so. Symbolically, it signifies that Christ inducts His people into the Kingdom of Heaven. St. Augustine is unique among the

Fathers in teaching that a Scriptural proposition may contain more than one *literal* significance. Of course it is evident that a sentence of the bible may be ambiguous and thus mean indefinitely many things; but that such a sentence without ambiguity may simultaneously and literally have many meanings, is commonly denied. For if that were the case, there could be no intelligent, unconfused, and certain understanding of the bible.

Scriptural inspiration demands, moreover, that the thought expressed in Scripture should coincide with the thought in its human author's mind; and that the thought in its human author's mind should be identical with the thought which its Divine Author wishes to express. For obviously, if the human author should not succeed in putting down on paper what he has in his mind, and if the Divine Author's ideas should be different from those of His human instrument, no amount of textual criticism could enable readers to know what the human and Divine Author wish to say. It would be as if the word "box" in the Gospel of St. Matthew meant a "blow in the face"; in St. Matthew's mind meant "box-wood," and in God's mind meant "a receptacle, for instance, for oranges." Thus who could learn from the Gospel of St. Matthew what Matthew and God meant by the word "box"? And so Scripture would be a closed book to the most analytic human scrutiny.

Finally, scriptural inspiration requires, over and above the fact that a book should be written by God, that it should also be committed to the Church as a deposit of faith for all Christians; for the Church has been appointed by Christ as the infallible custodian and expositor of His Word, without whom men cannot know it with certainty. The commission of the bible to the Church is, of course, subsequent to its composition, and hence does not constitute inspiration. But it is a necessary condition for the intelligent bestowal of the holy book upon men as a norm of faith.

It is clear, then, that if any of the books of the bible have been lost, they are not inspired in the strict sense of the word. For scriptural inspiration, strictly so called, signifies not only that a book is written by God, but also that it is actually in the hands of the Church. Were some scriptural books lost? Possibly. Will they be found? Possibly.

If found, can they contradict the Church's teachings? No; because her teaching is infallible. If found, can it be discovered that those books were written after the time of the Apostles? No, because as Catholics and Protestants teach, all scriptural inspiration for the Church at large came to a close with the death of John the Evangelist. Within the past few years a book was published with the title, "The Lost Books of the Bible." They were only apocryphal books long since rejected as spurious by the Church. Hence they were not lost, they were only ignored.

So far, therefore, we have been considering what is not *sufficient* to constitute scriptural inspiration. Let us now glance at what is not *requisite* for scriptural inspiration.

Ecstasy is not requisite for inspiration. Some of the prophets undoubtedly were rapt when writing their books or uttering their maledictions and promises. But it is evident from their own testimony and from their style of composition that other authors of the bible were in an equable condition of mind while composing. St. Paul was raised to the seventh heaven and St. John the Evangelist was ecstatic while visioning the Apocalypse. But those were cases of *revela-*

tion, not of *inspiration.* It is not at all evident that, when these two saints afterwards wrote down what they had seen, they were enraptured.

Awareness of inspiration, *i. e.,* the consciousness that one is inspired, is not requisite for an inspired scribe. Surely God could have exercised a secret, non-perceptible influence upon him. And this becomes more intelligible when we consider that divine, human, and diabolical impresses upon the mind do not by themselves give any clue as to the nature of their causes; just as typed letters on a sheet of paper before me do not show whether the keys of the instrument were pressed by a king, a philosopher, or a common crook. Nevertheless the Church knows that such parts of Scripture were inspired, on the authority of Christ and the Apostles. However, it is the opinion of the best theologians that, *as a matter of fact,* all the authors of Scripture were aware of their inspiration.

A divine facility in composition is not requisite for an inspired scribe. For while some of the authors of the Bible poured forth blazing thoughts with a passionate abandon and spontaneous fulness which were plainly superhuman, others had to labor industriously in gathering material for their books and putting it into readable form.

Originality is not necessary in an inspired book. Indeed the theory is admissible that Moses drew the materials of the Pentateuch from a tradition which had been the common possession of the Israelites for centuries before his time. It is even possible that Moses employed pagan documents. The pagans also had descended from some of the Patriarchs, had inherited their traditions and expressed them in books. True, these traditions had become corrupted with polytheistic ideas. But the substance of truth could have remained. Hence the objection so often drawn from the alleged fact that doctrines taught by Moses in the Pentateuch had been contained in pagan sources long before his time is futile. It was not necessary that the Pentateuch should have been original; what distinguished it from the pagan books was that, having been composed by Moses under the inspiration of the Holy Ghost, it forthwith became divine and infallible.

Privation of liberty in the biblical author

is not requisite for inspiration. Surely God had the power of inducing his human instruments (without *forcing* them) to write with infallible certainty all the things that He wished them to express. Therein lies the difference between a pen in one's hand and St. Matthew, for instance, in God's hand. For while the former must trace exactly what the writer wants, the latter was free to do otherwise; although he did infallibly write as God willed him to. As a matter of doctrine most theologians teach that the human authors of Scripture were free in God's hands. And they base their assertion on the general principle that, when God employs a human instrument, he employs him as he finds him. But the human instrument is naturally free.

It is not requisite that an inspired writer should have expressed himself with certainty. He could have done so doubtfully or with confessed ignorance, or even have given expression to emotions. God, the principal author of the bible, being infinitely wise and spiritual, cannot doubt, or be ignorant, or subject to emotions. When, therefore, God, the principal author of the bible, gives expression to these imperfect conditions of mind and heart, He means: "My human instrument, *e. g.,* Paul, doubts, is ignorant, feels sorrow, joy, hope or regret."

Beauty of material and perfection of style are not requisite elements in an in-inspired book. Just as the all-beautiful and perfect God was under no obligation to create a lovelier and more perfect world, than the one He did create, so He was not constrained to write a more perfect book than the actually existing Bible. As a matter of fact, while some portions of Scripture are sublime, simple and sweet, heroic, and tragic beyond words, other portions are prosaic and dull. Hence the foolishness of the fanatics who praise the stylistic qualities of Scripture without discrimination. Such people lay the artistry of Holy Writ open to attacks from profane critics who see plainly that secular literature surpasses portions of the bible.

Moral goodness in facts narrated is not requisite to the bible. In the histories of the Old Testament God narrates the misdeeds of the people of Israel. He does so disapprovingly. Had He approved of them, that would have been an argument against His holiness. It is obvious that God could not have composed an unclean poem, play or didactic treatise. Such compositions would imply corruption in their Author. However, it would have been permissible for God to record as a matter of history, not approvingly of course, that evil poems, plays and didactic treatises had been written by someone else in the past. In regard to the maledictions in the bible, it must be remembered that most of these were not curses, but prophecies of future direful events. For example, David did not curse his enemies, but merely foretold that they would be punished. It would have been wrong for him to exult in their punishment, but it was right for him to rejoice in the vindication of God's law *through their punishment*. God Himself may not take pleasure in the sufferings of unrepentant sinners, but He may take pleasure in the visitation of His justice upon those who obstinately refuse to be touched by His mercy. But after all has been said, it must be admitted that the manifestation of God's avenging wrath in the Old Testament was far less perfect than that of His loving kindness in the New. Then, the same flower which gives honey to the bee distills poison for the spider. And so, although the bible is good and holy in itself, it can be the occasion of harm to those who read it curiously or with a salacious mind. That is why the Church has never been in favor of the indiscriminate reading of the bible; and why, perhaps, the irreverent members of the Association for the Advancement of Atheism find the clear spring of Scripture a polluted puddle.

Material truth is not requisite to the bible. This brings us to the distinction between the truth of a citation and the truth of the thing cited. If Scripture attributes a saying to someone, it must be true that he said it; but Scripture does not vouch for the truth of what he says. Citations in Scripture are either implicit or explicit, either approved by God as true, or repudiated as false, or treated neutrally. Of these we shall speak more in a later lecture. An example of a Scriptural citation implicitly rejected by God as false is the text: "The fool hath said in his heart, there is no God." Since Scripture attributes this affirmation to the fool, obviously the fool said it; but it does not follow that the fool is right.

Verbal inspiration is not necessary in the

bible. The question of the inspiration of the material words of Holy Writ has been left open by the Church. However, one of the declarations of the biblical Commission seems to imply that the material words of Scripture are not inspired. For to the question: "Is it permissible for a Catholic to hold that the Pentateuch of Moses was not composed personally by him, but by a group of *uninspired* scribes and secretaries, who, under his direction, wrote down all those things, and those things only, which, under the inspiration of the Holy Ghost, he had conceived in his mind?" The answer was given in the affirmative.

There are still other arguments. For instance, Christ and the Apostles, when quoting from the Old Testament, are careful of the thoughts, but not of the exact words. But they would have been meticulously careful also of the words if the words had been inspired. Moreover a correct translation of the bible contains the inspired word as much as does the bible in its original language. But this would not be the case if the *words* of the original had been inspired. For the words of the translation are not the same as those of the original. They have identical signification, but they are different vocables in a different tongue. Again, authorship is complete without verbal expression. A secretary writes down in her own language the epistolary ideas of her employer; yet the resulting letter is not the secretary's, but the employer's. Then the style of Scripture is protean. Isaias is sublime and joyous. Jeremias is sad. Job is highly poetical. The author of the Book of Numbers is merely statistical. The Book of Kings accords perfectly in style with the primeval violence which it portrays. The Psalms are lyrical. The Gospels have the strength of simplicity. St. Paul's letters vibrate with passionate emotions. St. John's Gospel and the Apocalypse are the jewels of love and symbolism. How explain this variety of style? The most natural explanation is that, while God inspired the thoughts of the bible, He left the expression of them to the natural and varied genius of His human instruments. But someone may urge that at least in Scriptural poems and orations verbal expression is an essential part of authorship, because poems and orations are forms of art, and art consists as much in the expression of a thing as in the thing expressed. Granting for the sake of argument that in Scriptural poems and orations God's inspiration extends to the very words; we hold that in other less artistic forms of composition found in the bible, for instance, histories, letters and didactic treatises, the essential idea of inspiration is verified without reference to words.

However, all Catholic theologians are agreed that even if God did not directly inspire the words of the Bible, he was at least bound to preserve His human authors by a special gift of infallibility from erroneous expression. Otherwise they could have misstated God's thoughts and, as a consequence, the bible would not necessarily be infallibly true.

Up to the present we have been considering what Scriptural inspiration is *not*. Let us consider for a moment what it *is*.

The Vatican Council says: "The Church considers the Books of Scripture to be sacred and canonical because, . . . having been inspired by the Holy Ghost, they had God as their author." Leo XIII, explaining these words, says in his doctrinal letter "*Providentissimus Deus,*" "By supernatural power God so moved and impelled [the human authors of Holy Writ] to write; He was so present to them that the things which He ordered, and those only, they first rightly understood, then faithfully willed to write down, and, finally, expressed in apt words and with infallible truth. Otherwise it could not be said that He was the author of the entire Scripture."

According to this letter, therefore, the three elements which positively constitute scriptural inspiration (over and above the commission of the bible to the Church, of which we have already spoken) are: 1st, God's direction of the human author's intellect; 2nd, God's direction of the human author's will; 3rd, God's preservation of the human author from erroneous expression. For if this threefold divine influence were absent, the resulting book would not be divine, but human, fallible, and possibly erroneous.

Hence we must consider the inspiration of the bible in this light: Just as a poet formulates a vision in his imagination, resolves to put it down on paper, then uses a pen for that purpose, so that the resulting poem is not the pen's, but the poet's: so God from all eternity had certain truths in His mind for His people, willed to publish them, then employed prophets, poets, historians, and evangelists to express them, so that the Bible is His composition, not that of His human instruments.

Oh, what a Book! There is also, of course, the book of nature. For there are sermons in stones and books in running brooks, woods are voluble, every leaf has a tongue, the tumultuous sounds of the sea are articulate for spiritual ears, and indeed the whole earth and sky and ocean are inscribed with revealing ink, and the revelation is of God. But as Newman and Francis Thompson said, the book of nature has never satisfied the yearnings of the heart; for, after all, through the book of nature God does not speak to us verbally. Nature is only an effect of His omnipotence. Now who has ever been tenderly touched by the thought of the Creator of the world, who contains in Himself in a preëminent way all the beauty, goodness, power, and wisdom of the world? Who could fall in love with the Great Originator of the universe, the Cause of all things, Himself uncaused, existing beyond the farthest star and in the remotest eons of eternity? The ancient philosophers were chilled by the thought of such a Deity. Like an aviator in the strange realms of the air, or a tourist on the bleak Atlantic, they did not feel at home with Him, and so returned to the cheery, homey environment of earth, dedicating their best energies to the solution of its mysteries. Some of them even became agnostics and atheists.

But in the bible God is not impersonal and remote. Rather, the Inscrutable speaks to us in an intimate human way. Look out into the starry sky to-night, and it will seem cold and sublime; but listen in on the radio, and forthwith the "vasty deep" becomes as a comfortable room full of exquisite music and the voices of friends. And so the bible is a sort of wireless receiver, which whispers to our attentive ears that the sublime Deity of the Heavens became a child in a crib and a man upon a cross. All Scripture centers around Christ. Poetry, historical narratives, didactic wisdom, legal principles, prophetic visions, eloquence, and romance are as thick and glowing in the bible as encrusting jewels on a golden cup; and they all unite in saying that the chilly Deity of the Heavens became a child in a crib and a man upon a cross. Custom has staled us to the wonder of it all. But, there it is, the story of the Bible, the story of the mercy of the Just One, the lowliness of Infinite Power, the human kindness of the Lord of Heaven. Then, the tremendous words, "I am who am," have been changed into: "Come to me all ye who labor and are heavily burdened, and I will refresh you"; "Though a mother should forget her child, yet I will not forget thee"; "I am the Good Shepherd"; "My yoke is sweet and My burden light"; "I have compassion upon the multitude"; "Let the little ones come unto me, and forbid them not, for of such is the kingdom of Heaven."

Now you see why the Church has held fast to the bible at any price, fought for it to the last ditch, and waged war against atheists who say that God does not exist, that the bible is a myth and Christ a mere man. For so long as this biblical idea of Christ, the merciful Son of God, remains in the world, there is hope for humanity; but let that idea be erased from the memories of men, and the race is doomed.

It is no wonder that St. John Chrysostom called the bible a treasure, a mine of wisdom, a letter sent by our Father from

Heaven to comfort and enlighten us in our exile.

It is no wonder that, from the earliest days of Christianity down to the present time, portions of the bible have been read in church every Sunday, and the pagan persecutors thought that stealing the bible from the faithful would hurt them worse than taking their lives.

It is no wonder, then, that monks and nuns of the Middle Ages expended their finest decorative artistry on the vellum pages of the sacred volume. Their scrolls, their garlands and festoons of flowers, their ribbons of purple and peacock green on backgrounds of silver, their golden oranges, quaint little animals and heads of angels and men, bordering and glorifying the holy text, were intended to be only faint symbols of the color, warmth, beauty, unction, tenderness and sublimity hidden within for discerning eyes and seeing hearts.

In the British Museum they preserve and treasure letters and documents of great men and women—of Bacon, Mary Queen of Scots, and Blessed Thomas More. Why make little of this document from Heaven? A few years ago a copy of Joseph Conrad's first novel sold for $100,000. What value do you think ought to be placed on the Book whose author was God? Why do people engross themselves in the literature of the day and ignore the literature of eternity? Why do scientists pore over the Book of Nature studying its mysteries from stones up to man, yet limit their knowledge of the Bible to its cover? Why do they scrutinize with microscopic attention the diamonds, rubies and sapphires on God's footstool, the earth, but never look up at His beautiful face? Why, indeed?

Brethren, read this book. Retire for a time from the sordid world. Capture precious moments of solitude. Mount to spiritual heights from which you can get a correct perspective of life. Traverse this garden of refreshment with its clear pools, flowers, fruits, and sweet music, where more intimately than God in the original Eden with Adam and Eve, Christ walks in conversation with His elect. Do this; then through His eyes and conversation you will catch at least a keyhole view of the heavenly country awaiting you.

THE INFALLIBLE TRUTH OF THE BIBLICAL HISTORIES

To-night we ask whether the Bible, by virtue of its divine inspiration, is, in its historical books, infallibly true. Truth is moral or logical. The moral truth of the bible is opposed to mendacity. It means that the bible contains no lies. The logical truth of the bible is opposed to error and means that the bible contains no mistakes. According to the Modernists biblical history is true, not because it is a record of facts and objective truths, but because, 1st, it satisfies the religious needs of its readers and, 2nd, because it is a true expression of its writer's religious feelings and imaginations about facts or objective truths. Hence Scripture is a conglomeration of myths, legends, personal idealizations, and subjective exaggerations of facts and objective truths. For example, the Christ of St. John's Gospel historically speaking was no more than man. St. John idealized Him into a God.

According to the Orthodox the history of Scripture, quite apart from its authors' subjective state of mind and its readers' religious needs, is a true representation of things which really occurred. For instance, Christ was precisely as St. John portrays Him.

In recent times some few Catholics believed that Scripture is not true because its Divine Author, though incapable of error Himself, employed instruments of composition who were subject to error; and that as a matter of fact they, like defective pen points, marred the true character of God's Book. And they tried to prove their assertion by a parallel. God, they urged, said in the bible more than once, "I am ignorant, I doubt," not indeed because He was subject to these defects, but because some of His human instruments were ignorant or doubted. In a similar manner Scriptural error can be attributed to God, the principal author of Scripture, not because God could make a mistake, but because His human instruments could. But there is no parallel in the case. For whereas an ignorant man says: "I do not know"; and it is true that he doesn't know; an erring man says: "I know"; and it is false that he knows. Hence, while God without detriment to His veracity, can sponsor the assertion of one who confesses ignorance or doubt, He cannot back the statement of one who errs.

An objection to the veracity of Scripture sometimes takes this form: Attributing a book of Scripture to an author who did not really write it is a form of deceit. But such cases occurred in the bible.

It all depends on whether readers of the bible are aware of the fictitious character of such authorship. In the case of Ossian's poems, for instance, the reading public was deceived, thinking that they were enjoying the songs of an ancient Celtic bard instead of the clever imitations of McPherson, a modern Scotchman. Chatterton also was a literary forger who fooled the people. But if fictitious authorship is known to be such, there is no place for the charge of mendacity. Even we in modern days are accustomed to authors writing under a nom-de-plume. Now in ancient Jewish times the custom of attributing one's composition to some great sage, long dead, prevailed, was understood by everybody as a mere literary form, and so did not mislead. So much for the *possibility* of fictitious authorship in Holy Writ! As to the *fact,* the biblical Commission has declared that the Pentateuch, assigned to Moses, was really composed by Moses, if not verbally, at least according to substance and material; that it is not necessary to hold that all the "Psalms of David" were composed by David; that the second part of the Book of Isaias, assigned by some critics to a contemporary of the Babylonian Captivity, who was supposed to have lived and written hundreds of years after the time of Isaias, must be held to have been the genuine work of Isaias, equally with the first portion of the book of that name; that the four Gospels were written by Matthew, Mark, Luke, and John; that the time order of their composition was the same as the above order of their names and that Mark did not write the first Gospel from which the other three Evangelists drew theirs as from a common source.

But the bible is not only morally, it is also logically true. It is not only free from lies, but also from mistakes. There are many kinds of logical truth in Holy Writ: didactic truth, contained in books which faithfully explain moral, religious or philosophic principles; poetic truth, which truly represents artistic beauty; romantic truth, which, though not a picture of real characters and events, is nevertheless ideally true, *i. e.,* true to the possibilities of persons and events; the truth of parables, which are not narratives of things really occurring, but aptly illustrate a doctrine; the truth of history, which must be a veracious record of real happenings.

To the question: May there be parables in Scripture? we must answer, yes. For, as we have seen, parables have their truth; and it is commonly conceded that the Prodigal Son, the Good Shepherd, the Good Samaritan, and Dives and Lazarus are parables, narratives which do not recite facts, but illustrate the mercy, pity and justice of God.

May Judith, Tobias, Esther, and the Second Book of Machabees be regarded as parables? In regard to the *antecedent* possibility of this, there seems to be no reason against the view; for if a short narrative can be a parable, why not a long one? A necessary condition, however, for the writing of parables would be the obligation on the part of their author to make it clear to prospective readers that a parable, not history, is being told.

As to the *fact,* however, it is the common opinion of theologians that those four books are not parables, but histories. The biblical Commission has decided that it is not permissible to consider Judith, Tobias, Esther, and Machabees as parables, except for grave reasons. The Commission's declaration is not infallible; but it is the teaching of expert Scriptural scholars who form a part of the teaching Church. The Commission does not explicitly state that these books are historical, nor even that the arguments against them are lacking in solidity. Hence a Scriptural student may possibly discover solid reasons against their historicity and hold them to be parables. But he would not be allowed to teach that doctrine publicly as long as the decree of the Commission stands. The ordinary faithful who, speaking generally, are not familiar with the reasons for and against, are obliged to hold, at least provisionally and for the present, that these books are historical. Now in this matter the Church is not arbitrary. In view of the wholesale assaults made on Scripture by

Modernists during the past few years, she had to establish a tribunal to safeguard the Word of God, and just as true Americans loyally accept the decisions of the Supreme Court in regard to the Constitution of the United States, even though that Court is not infallible, so it behooves us to submit to the teaching of the biblical Commission, even though, absolutely speaking, the Commission can err.

A question of graver importance is this: May one hold that books of Scripture which are admittedly historical, not only in form but also in fact, contain, (mixed up with facts,) legends, fables, popular traditions, narratives not according to facts but according to appearances, citations from non-inspired writings, for the truthfulness of which the sacred authors give no guarantee; and prophecies which narrate future events without any regard for the time or order of their occurrence.

You see that now we are in the thick of the battle raging around Scripture to-day. The Modernists, of course, give a liberal answer to all these questions, reducing the bible to the level of a purely mythical tale. On the other hand, the Fundamentalists stick to the letter of the law which killeth. Forgetting the spirit which quickeneth, they have by their narrow-minded interpretation exposed the bible to the mortal attacks of scientists. The Scopes trial at Dayton, Tennessee, was an example of their excessive literalism. The head of the Doweite sect at Zion City, Illinois, has gone even farther than the Southerners, teaching that the sun moves relatively to the earth, that the earth is stationary and flat, that the world was made in six days of twenty-four hours each, and that evolution, considered even as a theory, is false and absurd.

The Church follows the golden mean between fanatical excesses. I do not promise to answer all the proposed questions adequately and in detail. Only a mountebank, after the manner of a quack doctor or shyster lawyer, would be so presumptuous. The study of the bible is not yet finished. Catholic scholars are working at it night and day. They have told us something of it; there is far more in reserve. Let us accept with gratitude what has been offered and wait patiently for what is still to come. Above all, let us not be hasty in adopting extreme views.

In a *narrative according to appearances* the author does not tell what really happened, but what appeared to happen. May such narratives be admitted in Holy Writ?

In regard to physical phenomena, *i. e.,* facts of physics, chemistry, astronomy, geology, etc., yes! In regard, however, to historical facts, no! For, in the first place, Scripture does not propose to teach the physical sciences. It leaves that work to scientists. Its task is the salvation of souls. Secondly, narratives according to appearances are commonly understood by people in their loose descriptive character when there is question of physical phenomena. For instance, even to-day, when it is known that the sun does not move relatively to the earth, we speak of the sun "rising" because it appears so to us; and nobody is mislead by our words. Surely, the same latitude of expression ought to be allowed the authors of Holy Writ when there is question of physical phenomena. Third, physical facts, as distinguished from physical appearances, can be discovered in their real character also from sources other than Holy Writ, *e. g.,* from the laws of physics, astronomy and biology. Fourth, the facts which Scripture wishes to teach can be disentangled from enclosing extraneous modes of expression, like grains of wheat from their shells. For instance, from the first three chapters of Genesis the Church has picked out these solid verities: God is one, not many; He created heaven and earth; He made Adam head of creation and drew Eve from his side; He placed them both in a garden of delights, where they sinned and whence they were expelled with the burden of original sin upon themselves and their progeny for all time. For these reasons, narratives according to appearances do not cause either ignorance or deception in the minds of readers, when there is question of physical phenomena, and hence, are reconcilable with Scriptural inspiration and truth.

Inversely, narratives according to appearances are not admissible in an inspired history of the *free acts of God and men.* For, first, Scripture in its historical books does explicitly propose to teach us the doings of God and men; second, narratives according to appearances which do not tell us of the facts, but only of factual appearances, *i. e.,* popular traditions about facts, are not in common use in real histories and are not generally understood by readers in their loose descriptive sense. Rather, in a strict history it is expected that expressions should be used in a literal sense. Exceptions, of course, are possible; but an exception proves the rule. Third, historical narratives are the only source from which human and divine events of the past can be learned. For instance, we could never discover from biology that Moses led the people of Israel out of Egypt. If, therefore, Scriptural narratives are only a gathering of popular traditions and poetic exaggerations of facts readers of the Bible would be left in ignorance of the facts and would be led into error by Almighty God Himself, the author of the bible.

These two consequences of ignorance and error, direful enough when there is only question of the more or less secular history of the Jewish people, would be intolerable in regard to those sacred narratives which are the foundation of our faith. For instance, if the account of Christ's life were not a literal record, but a popular exaggeration, Christianity would be a hollow mockery. *A fortiori,* legends, myths, folk lore, which have little if any foundation in reality, must be excluded from Holy Writ.

Having safeguarded the bible from such extravagant imputations, we may now ask, in a spirit of reasonable concession: Is nothing to be allowed to the naïve method and manner of narrative undoubtedly prevalent among the ancients? Must we suppose that they wrote history with scientific exactitude, without putting any personal color into their work? What they narrated must be true; but need the manner of their narrative correspond exactly with the manner in which the narrated things occurred?

Fundamentalists make no allowance here. But the Catholic Church does. For instance, the words, "God said, let there be light," according to the Catholic Church do not mean that God literally spoke those words. God has no lips or mouth wherewith to speak. Then, putting speeches into the mouths of characters who really never spoke them, though they had the ideas in their head and acted upon them, was a common literary form among ancient historians. The Roman historian Livy is an example. And so such speeches in Scripture would not be an offence against the truth. However, the biblical Commission declares that our Saviour really gave the sermon after the Last Supper, though perhaps not in the exact words quoted by St. John. Then, too, the creation of the world in six days may be considered a graphic method of expression; not as if God did not perhaps consume centuries in bringing the world to its present elaborate condition.

But it is not always easy to draw the right distinction between the narration of facts and the manner of narrating them; between substantial history and mere literary form; between objective verities and an author's personal coloring. Father Christian Pesch, S.J., has formulated a rule for this. He supposed as a necessary condition for the proper use of the rule that the critic can and does know the purpose, the design of a Scriptural book. And, indeed we are perfectly aware, for instance, that the purpose of the first three chapters of Genesis is to establish the truths referred to above regarding the origin of the world and the human race. Again, we can know that the whole of the Old Testament was designed to show the special supernatural providence of God over the people of Israel. Now, the rule may be stated thus: Whichever parts of a Scriptural book are necessary to bring out the design, the purpose of that book must be considered as substantial narrative. Other parts may be regarded as only methods of expression, subjective influences which the author introduces to adorn his narrative. It is obvious that this rule allows considerable latitude in interpreting Holy Writ and is far removed from the constraining formalism of the Fundamentalists.

The Instituto Biblico Pontificio of Rome, under the patronage of the Pope, is perhaps the foremost Scriptural school of the Catholic world. Pope Pius X founded it at the time of the condemnation of Modernism, to insure conservative Scriptural interpretation for the Church. The succeeding Pontiffs, Benedict XV and Pius XI, confirmed his appointment. While stopping at the Institute last year, I had an opportunity to propose a few questions to the Professor of the Old Testament. He told me, for instance, that it is permissible for a Catholic to believe that the waters of the Red Sea did not part for the Israelites. A wind blew the water of the sea back a distance from the shore; the Israelites passed dry shod and the waters returned to their place in time to drown the Egyptians. Manna did not fall from heaven, but was a plant which grew in the desert in such abundance that it supported the people of God for forty years. These and like interpretations may be given, *provided* we keep in mind that God exercised a very special providence in causing the wind to rise and fall propitiously for the Israelites, destructively for the Egyptians; and in making the desert extraordinarily fruitful for Moses and his followers. This is the utmost that can be granted against some prima facie meanings of Holy Writ.

In view of the difficulty of answering objections to the historical truthfulness of the Old Testament, some Catholic theologians excogitated the theory that much of the Old Testament is a congeries of citations from uninspired writers, for the truthfulness of which the authors of the bible give no guarantee. Thus, to the objection, "The bible contains errors," they give this easy answer: Yes, the bible is full of errors, but they are not due to the authors of the bible; they are quotations made from uninspired sources, without approval.

Obviously, such an explanation is too easy

to be true. It would imply, for instance, that God foolishly and deceptively wrote a history, the bulk of which His people could not accept as true; and that the Church was wrong when, in the Council of Trent, she taught that the whole bible with all its parts is sacred and canonical. Of course, there are citations in Holy Writ, some explicit, some implicit, some approved as true, others repudiated as false, and still others treated neutrally by the inspired authors. Each one of these must be studied individually on its own merits. But to admit this is not the same as to accept the wholesale theory of textual nullification just referred to.

Since prophets wrote poetically, they do not misrepresent the truth when they foretell future events without adverting to the temporal order of their occurrence. For instance, Christ prophesied the destruction of Jerusalem and the end of the world as if these two events would occur at one and the same time. At least many of the first Christians took that meaning from His words. Yet Christ, seeing the future in the manner of a vision, spoke truly. The biblical Commission denies that St. Paul taught that the end of the world was near at hand. However, it may be conceded that perhaps St. Paul thought the end was coming soon. The point is that, if he did entertain that idea, he did not express it under the inspiration of the Holy Ghost. The Holy Ghost made Himself responsible for all the Scripture that Paul wrote, but not for all that Paul thought.

The bugbear of Fundamentalists is Evolution. Evolution was probably suggested as a theory by St. Augustine in the fifth century, and is at best no more than a theory to-day; for the missing link has not been found. The curse of it is that popularizers of Evolution, like H. G. Wells, write of an evolutionary world as if it were a sober fact. They tell us, for instance, of the Piltdown man as if they had actually seen all the members of his anatomy. But numbers of reputable scientists feel that those highly prized prehistoric skulls and bones are not missing links at all, but remnants of a low type man or beast. According to such distinguished men as Virchow, Bateson, Romanes, Fleischmann, Hartman, and Robin, Darwinian Evolution, with its natural selection and survival of the fittest, is defunct even as a theory.

Yet we hear parvenus in the field of

science dogmatizing about Darwinism. Evolution is at best only a theory, but if it were a certainty, could it be reconciled with the bible? With the Fundamentalist interpretation of the bible, no! With the Catholic explanation of the bible? If we except extreme evolution, which denies the existence of God and the immediate creation of the soul by divine power, yes! For reason and revelation are alike from God, who is infinite in knowledge and veracity; therefore, findings from both sources must be true, and truth cannot contradict truth.

And now I imagine a Catholic exclaiming: How fortunate I am to belong to the Church! To be certain is the highest perfection of the mind. To be certain even of the multiplication table is thrilling. It is the fashion to-day for people to pose as sceptics. Scepticism is one of the most unnatural forms of human decadence. One might as well boast of being blind. In the field of morals the greatest of the ancient philosophers were pitifully circumscribed in their knowledge. The Church came on the scene, not hesitant, apologetic, and diffident; but decisively and confidently saying: Things are thus and so. She took the bible, separated what is literal in it from what is figurative, and gave us what must be believed. Consequently, in spite of the fluctuating opinions and destructive criticism of Modernists we can say forever with full assurance: I believe in the bible, as explained by the Church.

But while we Catholics are obliged to accept the Church's explanation of the bible, we are free to reject a variety of so-called biblical facts of Fundamentalism which are only stylistic ornaments. It may hurt us to part company with them because they are so beautiful; but their retention would expose us to legitimate attacks from scientists. We can take this consolation to our hearts, that the most touching beauty of the Bible, that of the Son of God made man for us will always remain literally true.

Oh, it is hard to be a Catholic, but it is satisfying and safe. It is more thrilling to be a freelance fighting single-handed, but it is more assuring to belong to an army submitting to discipline. It is more daring to try to cross the ocean in a skiff, but a normal man prefers one of the greyhounds of the sea. We tour continents on sumptuous trains, in sleeping cars, parlors and dining rooms; but to enjoy these luxuries we must submit to the constraint of being narrowed in our movements by the parallel rigidity of tracks, we must avoid the engine, obey conductors, and accept régime. And so travelers to the heavenly port on the ship of Peter sail safely, even luxuriously; but they have to pay for it by mounting a steep gangway and keeping their hands off compasses, tillers, and sails. All high things in life are conditioned by submission to law. Free-love and free-thought alike bore with satiety, take the glamour off romance, reduce form to loose flabbiness, and change well regulated liberty into license. High romance consists precisely in being confined to one lover; high thought, in being limited by the demands of the one beloved, which is truth. Meritricious love and unruly thought belong to the same category of conventional mediocrity. The unusual, the extraordinary, the breath-taking things of life have always been strangely under lock and key, bound down by iron-clad regulation, springing into the beauty and fragrance of fruition precisely because, like the seed in the dark dank ground, they have first been subjected to pressure, kept in abeyance, ruled and restrained.

And so, while I see clever critics exercising their personal ingenuity and private judgment in eviscerating the lovely figure of the Bible and stuffing it with the excelsior of rationalistic interpretation, I am not jealous of their vaunted freedom. Rather, I am proud of being under the tutelage of another critic, or rather an appraiser, the Church, who only strips Scripture of its literary garment so as to show us the radiant whiteness of its divested beauty and truth.

THE OBSCURITY AND INSUFFICIENCY OF THE BIBLE

We have seen that the bible, by virtue of its divine inspiration, is infallibly true in its historical books. To-night we ask whether the bible, by virtue of its inspiration, is perfectly clear and sufficient for the economy of Christianity.

Protestants in the past have held that the bible is perfectly clear because God, its chief author, is a person of infinite clearness in thought and in expression, and hence the bible, His composition, must be as transparent as crystal. Moreover, the bible is the only means of salvation and so must be free from obscurity.

Catholics hold that the bible is partially obscure. For while God's mind and expression are like the sun when He speaks to us directly without the mediation of men, His thoughts will lack clearness in their utterance if His human instrument of expression is obscure; just as the rays of the sun are dimmed by a soiled piece of glass through which they pass. For instance, the prophet Jeremias was rude in expression, Isaias was a genius. Hence God's ideas would be clearer in Isaias than they are when He speaks through Jeremias. Add to this that the bible is not the only means of salvation and its obscurities are compensated for by clear tradition.

The immediate followers of Luther, seeing the difficulty of defending the thesis that the bible is unqualifiedly clear, drew a distinction. The meaning of Scripture is obvious to the initiated, to the clean of heart; but not so to others. However, the early Reformers, each claiming for himself the spirit of God in abundance, read contradictory meanings into the sacred text. Then, how can anyone know with certainty whether, while reading the bible, he is under the influence of God's spirit, his own, or the devil's. So-called inspiration is a very subtle thing which foils the keenest analysis. The saints have always been suspicious of the spirit that moved them, for they knew that Satan assumes the character of an angel of light and that auto-suggestion palms itself off on its dupes as an operation of God. The best judgment that one can form of inspirational phenomena, even with the aid of external advice and expert direction, is that *probably* the Holy Spirit is at work in the soul. Moreover, according to this theory, Scripture is not clear to the uninitiated, to pagans, infidels and sinners in general. But, according to Protestants, the clear teaching of the bible is the only means of salvation for such.

The third theory was that Scripture is indeed clear, but presupposes an equipment of learning in its readers. The obvious answer is: What of the ignorant, for whom Scripture has a message as well as for the learned? And is it not true that the bulk of Christ's followers were ignorant and poor? That the bulk of the Church are poor and ignorant? And is it not also true that, in spite of their ignorance, they have spiritual sight and that knowledge often closes the eyes of the learned.

A fourth theory was that the bible is clear in matters necessary for salvation. Hence, when it is obscure, it is dealing with non-essentials.—But for the past four hundred years interminable controversies have been waged as to what is essential to salvation. Some Protestants have gone so far as to say that all things necessary for salvation are clearly expressed in the sentence: "Thou shalt Love God above all things and thy neighbor as thyself." If so, a very small portion of Scripture is clear. And is it not possible that what Scripture expresses obscurely, may be clearly laid down in Tradition as an absolute necessity?

Even to-day some Protestants teach that Scripture is perfectly clear. Others admit that it is partially obscure, and others cynically say that it is as clear as day that Scripture is not the Word of God at all, but is full of myths and mistakes and hence ought to be consigned to the rubbish heap of dead and forgotten books. Reason, they say, led the ancient world to the pinnacle of civilization. Then the bible was palmed off on a credulous world as the great enlightener. It has caused endless confusion and controversal bitterness. Let us, therefore, do away with it and restore reason. There is a degree of plausibility in this reasoning, but two important factors have been forgotten. First, the bible in the hands of the Catholic Church, far from breeding confusion, has been the foundation of a consistent doctrine. Second, reason can never completely satisfy the needs of men. It could not do so of old. The ancient civilization shone for a while, and then decayed. But why look back to antiquity? Did we not have in the late Great War the best example of the insufficiency of reason without religion for life?

In contradiction to the Protestant view on the clearness and sufficiency of Scripture, I hold with the Church that Scripture is partially obscure and insufficient for salvation. This statement means four things: first, it is not clear from the bible alone that the bible is even an authentic historical document; second, it is not clear from the Bible that the whole bible is inspired; third, the bible is not clear to most of us on account of our ignorance; fourth, quite apart from our ignorance, portions of the bible are not clear in themselves.

Historical authenticity embraces integrity, genuineness, and authority. A book has the quality of integrity if it is substantially the same to-day as when it was written. A book is genuine if it was really written by the authors to whom it is attributed. It is authoritative if its authors knew what they were writing about and told truly what they knew.

Now is it evident to you that this book, the bible, is substantially the same to-day as when it was written? that textual corruptions have not crept into it through the centuries? that those who transcribed it from manuscript to manuscript in innumerable copies, some of the manuscripts being almost illegible, did not either intentionally or unintentionally make a mistake? Is it evident also that the multitudinous translations of the bible are correct? Most certainly not.

Is it evident to you from this bible in your hands that this bible was really written by those to whom it was attributed? that the authors of the four Gospels, for instance, were not impostors who forged the names of Matthew, Mark, Luke, and John, pretending that they lived in the time of Christ, heard His words and saw His works, whereas they were of a later century? Multitudes of apocryphal works, spurious gospels, existed in the early days. The Church rejected them. Are you sure from the bible that these four Gospels are not apocryphal? Most certainly not!

Is it evident to you from this bible in

your hands, that this bible has the quality of authority? that its authors knew what they were writing about and told us truly what they knew? that they did not mistake the doctrine of Christ, imagining that He claimed to be the Son of God, whereas He taught He was only a man; and that His works were supernatural wonders whereas in fact they were only natural? And is it not possible that they wished to deceive us, mendaciously foisting a false religion on a credulous world? Is it evident from the bible that the bible has the quality of authority? Most certainly not!

This, therefore, is what we mean by saying that it is not evident from the bible itself that the bible is an authentic historical document with the three qualities of integrity, genuineness, and authority.

In the second place it is not evident from the bible itself that the bible is wholly inspired. Non-Catholics hold the opposite view, for two reasons; first, because they hold that the bible testifies that the whole bible is inspired; second, because it is adorned with a variety of qualities which prove it undoubtedly divine.

But, as we showed in the lecture on canonicity, the bible does not testify that the whole bible is inspired. But granting for the moment, for the sake of argument, that the opposite is true, I ask, why should we accept the word of the bible? Would that not be sophistical? Observe! One doubts the inspiration of Scripture. To solve his doubt, he appeals to the very Scripture whose inspiration he doubts! Would that not be what the logicians call a "vicious circle"? That would be like saying: A is true because B is true. But why is B true? Ah, because A is true. Nor is it evident from Scripture, considered as an *historical* document, that the whole bible is inspired. For inspiration is a hidden thing in the inspired author's mind, not visible to the eyes of an historian. But perhaps the prophet or evangelist told the historian that he was inspired! But why should the historian take his word? The prophet or evangelist could have been deceived as to his inspiration; for inspiration is a subtle thing, which defies the closest analysis and is scarcely distinguishable from influences from the devil or self. Then, he could have lied to the historian so as to obtain the character of a great prophet or evangelist among the people of God. But can we not suppose the case of a prophet, for instance, so upright in character and solid in judgment that he was neither deceived himself nor deceived others in regard to his inspiration? Yes. Could we believe him? Yes; but in that case our belief in biblical inspiration would be based upon human authority, namely, the prophet's; whereas, according to Catholics and Protestants alike, our belief in biblical inspiration is based upon divine authority. So we cannot have faith (at least divine faith) in Scriptural inspiration, on the authority of Scripture itself.

The qualities of Holy Writ which, according to Protestants, prove the bible to be inspired, are chiefly these: antiquity, beauty, consistency in moral teaching, harmony, and personal inspiration.

But if antiquity is a sign of divine inspiration, the pagan books of Babylonia and Egypt were inspired from on High because they are as old and even older than the bible.

If beauty is a criterion of inspiration, then Plato's works are inspired, for they are very beautiful; whereas the Book of Numbers was not the handiwork of God, for there is nothing beautiful about it. Moreover, the beauty of Scripture may be due to the beautiful *revealed* truths contained in it and expressed without a special gift of inspiration, by the natural powers of the author. Now you will remember that revelation is not inspiration. As to the stylistic beauty of the bible! Some passages are not stylistically beautiful at all. Those that are, can either be explained by the natural genius of their authors or do not postulate either genius or inspiration. For their beauty consists rather in the absence of all literary ornament; it is the simple loveliness naturally obtainable by ordinary men who had been sublimed by union with God; like a plain glass vase made luminous by a light within it. Besides, according to non-Catholics, the beauty of the bible is perceived only by the initiated, the pure of heart; it is not perceived by sinners. Hence, to the latter it cannot be a criterion of the inspiration of Scripture nor, obviously, a means of salvation. Yet through inspired Scripture alone, say non-Catholics, can men be saved.

The high form of morality, consistently taught for thousands of years without flaw by Holy Writ, beginning with the first great lesson of one God, Creator of heaven and earth, and ending with Christ's sublime Sermon on the Mount, is unique in the literature of right living. But it does not postulate inspiration. It can be explained by a special gift of infallibility, by which God preserved the authors of Holy Writ from error in teaching morality. But infallibility is not inspiration!

By the harmony of Scripture is meant its unity combined with variety; its many dissimilar volumes, different in style, written by a variety of authors in different centuries and localities; histories, poems, didactic treatises, prophecies, visions and epistles—all enclosed under one cover, teaching the one lesson of Christ; the books of the Old Testament by anticipation and the books of the New Testament in retrospect. But up to the third century the volumes of the Bible were not contained in one book under one cover. On the contrary, they were separately scattered over the earth, mixed up and confused with a variety of apocryphal works. Hence, though they had the quality of multiple variety, they lacked that of unity. The Church gave them the quality of unity by rejecting the apocrypha and binding the genuine books of Scripture into one volume. It is obvious, therefore, that without this editing of the Church the unity, and therefore the harmony of Scripture could never have been known. Add to this that some of the apocryphal works, humanly speaking, would fit into the scheme of Scriptural books harmoniously, whereas some of the genuine books of Scripture could be dropped without notable loss of harmony.

Last of all, if the power of inspiring pious emotions and high thoughts in the readers of the bible constitutes Scriptural inspiration, then the "Following of Christ" by Thomas à Kempis was written by God and the Book of Numbers of the Old Testament was not. For the former is rich and the latter sterile in pious emotions and high thoughts.

In the third place the Bible is not clear to most of us on account of our ignorance. Hundreds of thousands of people cannot even read. Of those who can, only a handful are familiar with the Greek, Aramaic and Hebrew languages in which the bible was originally composed. Hence, the generality of men cannot compare those tongues with their own and discover whether translators of the bible, either intentionally or otherwise, made a mistake. Then languages grow and change in the course of centuries. During the short space of one hundred years the English language in America, chiefly through colloquialisms and slang has become quite a new language; so that an Englishman can hardly understand an American. Surely, then, Hebrew of later centuries must have differed widely from what it was in the time of Moses. And so an acquaintance with contemporaneous Hebrew would not help one much to understand the Hebrew of the Pentateuch. Moreover, the authors of the Old Testament wrote of environment, of historical, geographical, local, tribal conditions and peculiarities which were intelligible to their immediate readers, but are not so to us. Worst of all, the bible contains mysteries unintelligible to reason. It is clear, then, that current words of the ancient tongues in their ordinary sense could not express mysteries. They had to be given an arbitrary technical sense, or utterly new words had to be coined for the expression of mysteries. The result was ambiguity and confusion. For instance, some

Christians think that the Greek word *Presbytereus* means priest, others that it signifies only an elder. To some the Greek word *pistis* means faith, to others, only trust.

In the last place, quite apart from our ignorance, many portions of the bible are not clear in themselves. St. John's Apocalypse in its symbolism is mostly unintelligible. Parts of St. Paul's letters and the Book of Proverbs are obscure. If it were not for the obscurity of Holy Writ, so many contradictory doctrines would not have been drawn from the private interpretation of it.

Why is Scripture obscure? The Fathers say in order that it may be prized more, studied more deeply, and be understood with increasing luminousness down through the centuries. "Easily gotten, is easily forgotten," holds of the understanding of the bible as of all other things. Saints and sages have pondered the Holy Book from age to age; so has the Church. They could not glean its meanings at once. Therefore we have what is called development of doctrine; not, indeed, an increase of revelation, (which came to a close with the death of John the Evangelist;) but a more perfect comprehension of the meaning of Holy Writ in these later centuries than was had in olden times.

God may possibly have made Scripture obscure to confound the inquisitiveness of private judgment and to force men to have recourse to the authentic interpreter of the bible, the Church.

But the ultimate reason for the lack of clearness in Holy Writ was God's choice of human instruments of composition, with all their natural peculiarities and defects. Not all the authors of the bible were geniuses. Some of them were untutored and of middling artistic caliber. Hence portions of the bible are beautiful beyond words; other portions are rough and dark.

My non-Catholic brethren, I trust, will pardon me for pointing out the disastrous consequences which have followed from an exaggerated idea of the clearness of Holy Writ. Some people start out by assuming that the bible is as luminous as the sun. Then they discover to their dismay that it gives no guarantee of its historical authenticity, no sufficient guarantee of its divine inspiration, and in many places no guarantee even of its meaning. Accordingly, they become disappointed, chagrined, sceptical, critical and, in too many cases, reject the bible utterly. Others take the bible on faith without those reasonable proofs which every man has a right to expect. And having commenced by an arbitrary acceptance of it, they continue in an arbitrary interpretation of it, until they fall into a labyrinth of contradictory doctrines. The first Reformers derived the bible from the Catholic Church; and Protestants of to-day who do not concede that she preserved the Bible for them, cannot logically admit Scriptural historical authenticity at all. Happily for themselves, the majority are not logical, and still hold onto the bible after having lost their hold on the Church. This is well. But meanwhile they ought to think of their own glass houses when they are disposed to throw stones at what so many of them choose to call the lack of thought prevalent among Catholics.

The bible, like every other book, is a dead thing, requiring a living interpreter. Even the Constitution of the United States, in spite of its fundamental simplicity, needs the interpretation of the Supreme Court. Without the Supreme Court the Constitution would be given twenty different meanings in a year. What then shall we think of the bible, so ancient, so complex, so subtle, written by such a variety of authors in different languages, styles and centuries, and full of supernatural mysteries! The Church is a living interpreter, having about her all the interest which attaches to a vital thing. Any day she may come out with a religious declaration which will make us hold our breath at its daring and apparent novelty. The Old Man of the Vatican (if I may use the phrase with all reverence in regard to a figure of ancient dignity) seems somnolent for years, with a world of energy swirling and sweltering at his feet. Suddenly he bestirs himself, drops lethargy like an old cloak from his shoulders, shines in the young beauty of truth, dissipates mists of error, doubt and ignorance, and then falls back again into what seems to be sleep, but in reality is his ancient contemplative brooding over the written and spoken story of Christ's Life.

But it must be remembered that the Pope's teaching is not arbitrary. The Holy Father does not wake up of a morning, look out the window, rub his hands and say: "It's a fine day for a dogmatic declaration;

let us formulate a canon on Scripture or hurl an anathema or two against the Modernists!" On the contrary, a necessary condition for doctrinal teaching is that it can be traced back through the Fathers to the Apostles and to Christ. In this source, therefore, namely Tradition, the Pope finds the wisdom which compensates for the obscurity of Scripture. We ordinary Catholics must take our knowledge of divine things from the Pope, his Bishops and theologians at second hand, for the simple reason that we have not the time or the ability to read the bulky volumes of the Fathers. And here our non-Catholic friends appear to be inconsistent. For while they bow their heads to medical, legal, and scientific dogmatism, they suddenly stop at the authority of the Church. It is difficult to be docile to didactic authority, but docility has its reward. It is pleasant to be independent in judgment, but free-thought carries a curse. Catholics compensate for the darkness of Holy Writ by Tradition explained to them by the Church. But non-Catholics can never completely raise the veil from the obscure pages of Holy Writ.

THE BIBLE AND TRADITION

Since it is not clear from the bible itself that it is an authentic historical document and inspired by God; since the bible is not clear to most of us on account of our ignorance and many portions of it are not clear in themselves; it follows that the bible is not sufficient for the economy of Christianity, the salvation of souls. Something else is necessary, and that we call Tradition. Tradition is the spoken word of Christ and the Apostles, never committed to the bible; their oral teaching, come down to us through the Fathers and Councils, and explained by the Church.

When Christ sent forth His apostles for the conversion of the world, He did not say to them: "Write bibles and instruct the people to read them," but, "go forth and preach." St. Paul says, faith cometh not by reading but by hearing: and of the first disciples it was said they went forth *preaching* everywhere.

The first Christians depended exclusively on preaching for their salvation, for the simple reason that the New Testament had not yet been composed in their time. Therefore Tradition, established by Christ in the beginning, and necessary for the first Christians, was to be until the end of time a necessary means of salvation, unless it can be proved that Christ wished to supplant it with the bible. But there is not one jot of evidence for this. Christ said, go forth and preach to *all* nations. But all nations will not have been preached to until the end of the world. Certainly, at least all nations have not been preached to yet. Think of the hundreds of millions of Orientals still in the non-Christian religions. Moreover, Christ said; "Behold I am with you all days even to the consummation of the world,"—meaning obviously that He would be with them, and their successors helping them to preach, until the end of time.

Since, therefore, according to Christ, Divine Tradition will always be necessary for man, it was incumbent upon Him to establish a channel through which His unwritten teaching and that of the Apostles could be handed down to men through the future ages. He did so, and the channel was the Fathers and ancient councils of the Church.

The Fathers of the Church were a group of holy and learned men living from sub-apostolic times down to the ninth century, who spent their lives in studying and meditating on God's Word. Chief among them in the West were Augustine, Jerome, Ambrose, and Gregory the Great; in the East, John Chrysostom Basil, Gregory Nazianzen, and Athanasius. Surely these are names to conjure with. Learning, eloquence, sanctity, and genius are connoted by them. If to anybody, the unwritten Word of God could have been committed to them with safety. Now the councils took the vast learning of the Fathers and expressed it in neat compact sentences, like a lens drawing in the rays of the sun from the remotest stretches of space and focusing them in a point. Out of the Fathers and councils the Church draws her wisdom. Here, for instance, she discovers the Apostolic doctrine that the whole bible is inspired.

And, indeed, Protestants ought to admit that Tradition is necessary for the economy of salvation. For they along with Catholics practice a divine ordinance for which there is no authority in Scripture; namely, the change of the Sabbath from the divinely appointed Saturday to Sunday. The authority for that momentous transformation can be discovered only in the unwritten teaching of the Apostles or of Christ. St. John the Evangelist declares that if all the things Christ did and said were written, all the books in the world could not contain them. And it stands to reason that a slender volume like the New Testament, written almost casually at the request of various churches, cannot include the whole doctrine which Christ and the Apostles taught through many years of Apostolic work.

But Tradition is also *sufficient* for man. If the bible had never been written, not a whit of Christ's doctrine would have been lost; and if the bible perished to-day, and the memory of it vanished from the minds of men, we should still have in Tradition enough for salvation; because Tradition contains the whole deposit of faith of which the bible is only a written fraction.

But the bible is necessary for us in a certain limited sense. For it was obligatory for the first Christians to accept this wondrous gift from the hand of God, to preserve it incorrupt, to reverence it, to read it devoutly, to ponder it, to preach from it, and rather sacrifice their lives than lose it. For it is one of the most precious of God's gifts.

But though the bible is neither necessary nor sufficient to man, speaking generally; is it sufficient and necessary to prove that the Catholic Church is Christ's infallible representative upon earth?

It *is sufficient* for that. From the two texts: "Thou art Peter, and upon this rock I will build my Church, and the gates of hell shall not prevail against it; and to thee I give the keys of the kingdom of heaven, and whatsoever thou shalt loose on earth, shall be loosed in heaven; whatsoever thou shalt bind on earth, shall be bound also in heaven"; and, "Feed my lambs, feed my sheep," prove that Christ made Peter the head of His Church. But from history and the testimony of the Fathers it is clear that the Catholic Church is Peter's Church. For history traces back the unbroken line of the bishops of Rome from Pius XI to Peter and Christ; and the universal testimony of the Fathers is this: "You must obey the Bishop of Rome because he is St. Peter's successor."

But the Bible is not *necessary* to prove the fact. For quite independently of the witness of the Bible, two arguments, namely, the testimony of the Fathers and the miraculous character of the Catholic Church operating for over nineteen hundred years, establish the primacy of the Bishop of Rome. The latter argument is succinctly expressed by the Council of the Vatican; "The Church has within herself, by virtue of her wonderful spread, her great sanctity, her inexhaustible spiritual riches, and her unconquerable stability through the ages, four unanswerable motives of credibility which prove her mission from God." Since the Church is backed by God's own power, she shares in His infallible truthfulness when teaching *ex cathedra.*

Inversely, is the Church sufficient and necessary for the bible? She is *sufficient* for it because, without leaning on critics outside her pale, she is able with the help of her doctors and theologians to establish the historical authenticity and divine inspiration of the Bible and to explain its meaning in matters of importance with regard to salvation.

She is *necessary* for it because she is the only infallible teacher. It follows that no critic interpreting certain portions of the Bible by the light of private judgment can be sure he is getting the truth.

In regard to the relationship between Scripture and the Church we Catholics are sometimes accused of arguing in a vicious circle. People say: "You build the Church on Scripture and then turn around and build Scripture on the Church."

We do prove the Church from Scripture and Scripture from the Church; but under different respects. From the Church considered as an *historical witness* we prove that Scripture is an *historical document.* From Scripture as *an historical document* we prove that the Church is an *infallible teacher.* From the Church considered as an *infallible teacher* we prove that Scripture is *inspired by God.* By saying that the Church is an historical witness, we mean that she existed back through the ages to the time of Christ, saw the Evangelists writing their Gospels, was aware that they were Matthew, Mark, Luke, and John, that they knew what they were writing about and told us truly what they knew; and she preserved their composition from substantial corruption until the present day. When we say that Scripture is an historical document, we mean that what it says is true. Among other things Scripture states that there was a man named Christ, who strictly claimed to be the Son of God and proved the truth of His claim by undoubted miracles. Accordingly, whatever He taught was true with the truth of God Himself. But He taught that He would build an infallible Church upon Peter. From ecclesiastical history and the Fathers it is obvious that the Catholic Church is Peter's Church. When we say that the inspiration of the Scripture can be proved from the Church, we imply that it is a matter of faith. But Protestants as well as Catholics admit that this is so. Now the Church is infallible in matters of faith.

Someone may urge: It would seem from all you say that, according to Catholics, the Church is superior to the bible. Indeed, brethren, the contrast ought not to be drawn between the Church and the bible; but between the Church, plus Tradition, plus the bible; and the bible, plus private judgment. We hold that the former group of authorities is superior to the latter. Moreover,

Tradition, taken by itself, is superior to the bible because it contains the whole deposit of faith of which the bible is only a written fraction. The end is superior to the means. But the end of the whole economy of Christianity is the salvation of the Church and the children; the bible is only a means to attain that end. The Spouse of God is superior to the Word of God. But the Church is the Spouse of the Son of God; the bible is only His Word. The Church existed and functioned before the bible was written; indeed the bible was conceived in the bosom of the Church. In that sense, too, the Church is superior to the bible. The Church was more intimately divine in her origin than the bible. For the Church was founded directly by Christ, whereas the bible was written only through the mediation of men. The Church's teaching is clear and unmistakable, whereas the bible is obscure. Hence, while one who interprets the bible by private judgment can lose his faith, a follower of the Church in matters of doctrine can never go wrong. In these senses, if you will, the Church *is* superior to the bible.

But if our critics affirm that, according to Catholics, the words of the teaching

Church in conciliary chapters and canons and in doctrinal bulls are superior to the words of Scripture, they are mistaken. For we hold that the Church's teaching is only infallible, whereas the bible's is infallible and divine; her words are only man's, the bible's are God's; her documents are generally only clear, concise, and intellectual, whereas the Scriptural document is full of unction, savory wisdom, simple majesty, poetic colorfulness, moral suasion, eloquence and supernatural mysteries.

Indeed, we challenge anyone to show greater loyalty, admiration and respect for the bible than ours. For whether we consider its Author, its end and purpose, or its contents, we hold it to be the greatest book in the world.

Its author was God. What, therefore, from this point of view are the plays of Shakespeare, the Divina Commedia of Dante, the epics of Homer and Virgil in comparison with the bible! Its end and purpose are the glory of God and the salvation of men. How inferior to it are books of science whose end is only the knowledge of created truth and books of literature, whose sole end is the admiration of created beauty.

Its subject-matter is God, the Creator of Heaven and Earth, the Redeemer of the world and Sanctifier of men, and man in relation to this most Holy Trinity. Accordingly, it contains histories which, like Genesis, narrate and describe the creation of the world and the fall of man with a sublimity unsurpassed and which, like Exodus, show the providence of God over the people of Israel. It contains poems which, like the Psalms of David, go through the whole gamut of human emotions and intellectual aspirations with regard to God; and which, like Job, touch peaks of grandeur and depths of pathos. It contains books of morality which like Wisdom, Ecclesiasticus, and Proverbs, convey hard lessons sweetly with the "*utile dulci*" of the poet. It contains prophecies which, like the visions of Isaias and Jeremias, portray the glorious mysteries of our Lord's life with a golden joyousness and His sorrowful mysteries with a violet sadness. The New Testament contains histories like the four Gospels, which by their simplicity, sincerity, and dramatic movement have cast a spell over all succeeding ages. It contains didactic letters which, like St. Paul's, pulsate with love, fear, hope, and grief. It contains the Apocalypse of St. John, the vision of glory awaiting those who accept the leadership of Christ.

The central point of the whole Great Book is Jesus Christ; Christ, the Lover, who came down from Heaven to woo us; Christ, the Purifier, who died on the cross to cleanse us of sin; Christ, the magnetic Leader, who weaves the web of enchantment around whosoever ventures into the charméd circle of His spells; Christ, the Sender, who missions the Holy Ghost, the spirit of holiness to a needy world; Christ, the Founder of a spiritual empire, His Church, which in His name, by means of creeds, commandments, Mass, Sacraments and prayer, teaches, rules, and strengthens the faithful on earth in preparation for Heaven.

The Church appreciates this treasure in her hands. She received it from God with profound gratitude and reverence; she made sure of its genuineness and authority; she separated it from a route of forged gospels and edited it in its unique beauty; she translated it carefully for the advantage of her children; she transcribed it to pages of vellum and papyrus in inks of purple, crimson, and gold; she bade her great doctors, Augustine, Jerome, and Thomas spend the best energies of their mighty intellects and gifted tongues in expounding it to the people and defending it against its enemies; she watched night and day to protect it against the almost inevitable corruptions of nineteen centuries; she embodied its lessons in many colored mosaics, paintings, statues and windows of gorgeous hues; in our day, in the person of Leo XIII, she has written beautifully of its heavenly wisdom, unction, eloquence, poetry, and most dear mysteries; and in the person of Pius X she has fulminated her anathema against modernistic critics, because, less scrupulous than the soldiers at the foot of Christ's cross, who declined to rend His seamless garment, they have torn to shreds the resplendent imperial fabric of Scripture which enfolds Him.

Let us imitate the devotion of the Catholic Church to the bible! Let us read it, ponder it, steep our minds in its light, and saturate our spirit in its unction, so that, after the manner of St. Paul, each of us may exclaim: I live, now not I, but this book lives in me!

Then, in the everlasting mansion of the

King (in comparison with whose royal appointments the sky-colored green and violet hangings fastened with cords of silk, inserted into rings of ivory and held up by marble pillars; the floors inlaid with porphyry and white marble, and embellished with paintings of wonderful variety; the golden cups and sweet music of Balthasar's palace were tawdry and dull): in that home of the Blessed, with the King of Kings seated at the table's head, with no Daniel interpreting handwriting of doom upon the wall, we shall quaff forever, not sacrilegiously but reverently from the golden chalice of the bible the delicious wine of God's Truth, Wisdom, Goodness, Mercy, Beauty, and Love.